You can have more than one home. You can carry
your roots with you and decide where they grow.

—Henning Mankell

MYSTERIES OF COBBLE HILL FARM

MYSTERIES OF COBBLE HILL FARM

Three Dog Knight

JOHNNIE ALEXANDER

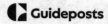 Guideposts

Cover and interior design by Müllerhaus
Cover illustration by Bob Kayganich at Illustration Online LLC.
Typeset by Aptara, Inc.

ISBN 978-1-961251-06-9 (hardcover)
ISBN 978-1-961251-45-8 (softcover)
ISBN 978-1-961251-07-6 (epub)

Printed and bound in the United States of America
10 9 8 7 6 5 4 3 2 1

MYSTERIES OF COBBLE HILL FARM

Three Dog Knight

GLOSSARY OF UK TERMS

A&E • accidents and emergencies (hospital department)

biscuit • cookie

boot • trunk of a car

car park • parking lot

casualty department • emergency room

chuffed • delighted, pleased

Cornish fairing • spiced ginger cookie

crisps • potato chips

cuppa • cup of tea

dustbin • garbage can

Empire biscuit • Scottish sandwich cookie with raspberry jam

fizzy drink • soda

jumble sale • garage sale; yard sale

jumper • sweater

ramble • walk in the countryside

snap • photograph

takeaway(s) • restaurants that offer takeout (food)

telly • television

torch • flashlight

wellies • Wellington boots

CHAPTER ONE

The brown-and-white Mini Lop rabbit, though wrapped in a fleecy doll blanket, shivered as Harriet Bailey passed him to young Winifred on this Tuesday afternoon in September.

The ten-year-old girl cuddled her new pet in her arms, holding him close as she stroked one of his silky-soft ears. The gesture reminded Harriet of another young girl who had often popped into her prior veterinary clinic with a rabbit or a hedgehog or an orphaned possum—whatever the child found in her countryside wanderings. Harriet never knew what to expect when the shoebox lid was dramatically lifted to reveal the injured creature inside.

Both girls had blond hair, intense blue eyes, and sharp features. They might have been sisters, except they lived an ocean apart—one in rural Connecticut and this one on a farm a few miles outside the charming Yorkshire village of White Church Bay, England.

"It's an awful thing people do to these bunnies." Alma Wilkerson placed a comforting arm around her daughter's thin shoulders. "Buying them as pets then abandoning them when their tykes grow tired of caring for them. The poor things don't know how to live in the wild."

"At least this one has found a home." Harriet gave Winifred a reassuring smile while her insides burned with frustration. She'd recently found a year-old newspaper article in Grandad's archives about an area in West Yorkshire where rabbit rescue groups were overwhelmed with the problem. Apparently, the media attention had done nothing to curb the inhumane practice.

Harriet met Alma's gaze and prayed her well-intended words wouldn't cause offense. "A pet should never be an impulse," she said. "Though perhaps this one is an exception to the rule."

"That it is, and you needn't worry," Alma assured her. "We already have quite the menagerie at our place, and a more motley collection you've probably never seen. One more will make little difference. Why, it was my own boy, Walker, who brought Maxwell to Old Doc Bailey. We'd have kept him too, except Doc fell in love with the pup."

At the sound of his name, Maxwell's ears perked up. The black-and-tan long-haired dachshund had followed Harriet into the examination room and greeted the Wilkersons with happy barks. His back legs had been paralyzed when he was hit by a car, but Harriet's grandfather had outfitted him with a wheeled prosthesis, so the dog had little trouble getting wherever he wanted to go.

Now he was the official clinic dog—a fun surprise included in Harriet's inheritance of Cobble Hill Farm, which encompassed her grandfather's nineteenth-century house, art gallery, and veterinary practice. She'd also been given stewardship of Charlie, the official office cat. After she'd been rescued from a burning dustbin as a kitten, Grandad had adopted her too, making her the latest in a long line of clinic cats named Charlie. Harold Bailey had always insisted that giving them all the same name gave him one less thing to remember.

Charlie's sweet temperament made her a delight to have around. Despite her physical scars, or perhaps because of them, the muted calico was one of the most affectionate cats Harriet had ever come across.

"Grandad enjoyed Maxwell's company," Harriet said. "And I do too." Especially on those occasional evenings when Connecticut felt as distant as the moon and she second-guessed the wisdom of her radical move to Yorkshire.

"I'm naming him Toffee, and he'll stay in my room," Winifred asserted confidently. She focused her intense blue gaze on Harriet. "He'll be okay now, won't he?"

"You did everything you could for him," Harriet replied. "Keeping him warm, feeding him, and cleaning that nasty wound. And I've done everything I can."

"Giving him medicine," Winifred said.

"That's right." Harriet had treated the wound on Toffee's haunch and suggested vaccinations as well as an antibiotic. "So now it's up to Toffee to get better."

Winifred's features softened as a huge smile lit her face. Reassured that the Mini Lop had found his forever home, Harriet ushered the little girl and her mom from the examining room to the empty reception area. Maxwell dutifully followed behind them.

"I hope we didn't keep you from any plans," Alma said as she paid the bill. The Wilkersons had arrived with the injured rabbit a minute before the clinic closed. Polly Thatcher, the receptionist, usually locked up, but she'd already left due to an eye appointment.

"Nothing that couldn't wait," Harriet replied. "I'm closing early today because Aunt Jinny and I are taking items to the Antique Festival for the appraisal exhibit."

Harriet's paternal aunt, a local physician, lived in the dower cottage that had once been part of the farm. Her husband, Dominick, had died of a heart attack about ten years before, and her son lived with his wife and two children in nearby Pickering. The entire family had welcomed Harriet with open arms when she arrived.

"We're going to the festival too, aren't we, Mum?" Winifred practically bounced with excitement. "I'm going to ride the Ferris wheel and eat cotton candy and all kinds of stuff."

"That's for later," Alma said. "After the chores are done."

"And after I get Toffee settled," Winifred agreed more seriously.

"I was surprised when Aunt Jinny told me about the carnival," Harriet said. "When I first heard about the festival, I thought it was specifically an antique show."

"It started out that way." Alma tucked her debit card into her wallet. "Quite like the program on the telly where people bring in old items to see if they have any value. As the years went by, the committee added the rides, food vendors, and entertainment. It's all different than it used to be except for the name. That hasn't changed, but that's because of Ivy and Fern, the infamous Chapman sisters."

"I've met Fern but not Ivy." Harriet printed Alma's receipt and stapled it to her invoice.

"Those two are like oil and water. Always have been." Alma raised her eyes to the ceiling as if seeking divine guidance, and Harriet, who'd had her own entertaining interactions with Fern Chapman, hid a smile.

"Ivy has been on the Antique Festival committee since its beginning, and she came up with the name," Alma continued. "As the event became more successful, Fern insisted on being involved too. She couldn't let Ivy get all that praise year after year, could she?"

Harriet chuckled. "Some sisterly truths are universal."

"That they are. Anyway, each year Fern makes a motion at the planning meeting to change the name, and each year that motion goes down in flames. The other members vote against Fern to keep Ivy happy. They have to keep Fern happy too though, so when she makes a motion to add something new to the event, they agree. This year it's a dunk tank."

"That sounds entertaining." Though she wanted to be diplomatic, Harriet still found it difficult to reconcile Ferris wheels and dunk tanks with the upscale appraisal event she'd envisioned when she read the festival's promotional materials. Those hadn't mentioned carnival rides or fair food. Not that she was opposed to either.

"It's fun for the children," Alma agreed. "Even though Ivy's initial dream of a premier antique show with a national reputation gets dimmer while the event grows beyond the name, she's too stubborn to change it to something more fitting."

Harriet couldn't pretend to know the inner dynamics of the Chapman sisters' relationship, but her sympathies were with Ivy. The carnival rides and games were surely fun for the community, but Ivy must be disappointed to see her dream of an event that celebrated history and legacy overshadowed by something altogether different.

When Aunt Jinny invited Harriet to attend the festival with her, she'd mentioned that local residents often learned surprising historical details about the treasures stowed away in their attics. The previous year, Miss Jane Birtwhistle, retired schoolteacher and feline aficionado, had brought in a vase to be appraised and almost had a heart attack when the appraiser valued it at over five thousand pounds. Most items weren't worth nearly as much, except in sentimental value. Still, it was all good fun, and Aunt Jinny had encouraged Harriet to find something to take to the event.

Once the Wilkersons were on their way with cheery goodbyes, Harriet locked the clinic door and flipped the sign from Open to Closed. While she tidied up, she glanced at a decades-old photograph of Grandad, when his hair was still dark and he sported a moustache, standing beside a famed racehorse whose care had been entrusted to Old Doc Bailey and no one else.

Hundreds of similar photos were in albums of various sizes in Grandad's study—Old Doc Bailey with prize bulls and sheep, bottle-fed calves and foals, dogs, cats, guinea pigs, a variety of reptiles and birds, and even chickens—lovingly compiled by Grandma Helen, who had died of cancer before Harriet was born. Aunt Jinny had maintained the tradition of taking and preserving photographs of her father.

Perhaps Harriet should have taken a selfie of herself with Winifred and her new bunny. In the age of digital photographs, it might be nice to create photo albums of her own to add to the Bailey legacy.

She hung her white lab coat on its designated hook then opened the door connecting the clinic to the kitchen so Maxwell could enter in front of her. Though she'd moved to the farm a few months before, she still found it difficult to believe the stone Georgian-style house and all its contents belonged to her.

Of course, that meant all the inconveniences that came with outdated plumbing, heating, and electrical systems belonged to her as well. Strange how those issues that had seemed so overwhelming when she first arrived were now mere annoyances.

Though she loved everything about the decor of her new house, Harriet had added a few personal touches of her own, including a framed montage of five photographs that adorned an open space on the kitchen wall. She paused to soak in the memories ignited by those photos. Her favorite showed her parents standing beneath a giant sycamore tree on a beautiful sunshiny day. They'd been oblivious to the click of Harriet's digital camera as they shared the kind of smile that came with decades of happy marriage.

How she missed seeing them every day. The ache for home tugged at her heart, its suddenness bringing tears to her eyes. How could she have left Mom and Dad, everything she'd known and loved, to move thousands of miles away? At the time, when she was in such despair, the news of the inheritance had seemed an answer to prayer. An excuse to escape.

But ever since she'd received the invitation from the Whitby Women's Society to speak at their monthly luncheon in less than two weeks, she'd been bombarded with thoughts of what she'd left behind when she'd said goodbye. Her heart was heavy with a longing not only for a home but for *home*.

Going back, however, was impossible. How could she after Grandad had entrusted his beloved home, his veterinary practice with its odd assortment of eccentric clients, and his paintings to her keeping? She believed herself to be more of the steward of his legacy than the new owner of all that was once his, and she intended to honor and protect what he'd devoted his life to build and then passed along to her.

An ornate wall clock chimed the quarter hour, and Harriet jumped. She'd been so lost in her thoughts that the minutes had ticked by without her. She hurried to the entryway, where a golden umbrella stand, a porcelain peacock figurine, and a blue-and-white delft pitcher were displayed on a side table. Harriet had chosen each item as a possible contender, but she couldn't decide which of the three to have appraised at the festival.

A knock sounded on the door as it opened. "It's me," Aunt Jinny called. She smiled at Harriet as she entered the house. She wore a pale yellow sweater—which she would call a jumper—and pleated trousers. A blue-and-green paisley scarf completed the outfit.

"I'm sorry I'm running late," Harriet said. "I had a last-minute rabbit emergency."

"The Wilkersons? I saw their car pulling out and guessed you'd been held up. But I'm the last person you need to apologize to when it comes to medical emergencies." Though she was nearing retirement age, Aunt Jinny's family practice kept her busy. "I've lost count of the number of times I've missed the opening hymn at church."

"Winifred found a Mini Lop this morning by their mailbox," Harriet explained. "Poor little guy had a gash on his leg and was scared half to death."

"Are the Wilkersons keeping him?"

"Thankfully, yes, and Winifred has named him Toffee. She's taking his care very seriously. Otherwise, I suppose the clinic would have a new mascot. He's cute, but a clinic dog and an office cat are more than enough for me to keep up with, to say nothing of any boarders or overnight patients."

"Speaking of, where are Charlie and Maxwell?"

"I imagine Charlie is curled up in a patch of sunshine somewhere. And Maxwell headed to Grandad's study after the clinic closed. He likes lounging in there sometimes." Harriet waved at the side table. "Will you help me decide what to take to the festival? I thought the pitcher because it seems most likely to be worth something, but maybe not. I have no idea where it came from."

As an artist himself, Grandad had a keen eye and impeccable taste. But he also had a playful, whimsical side and was known to browse what the British called jumble sales for anything that caught his eye, even if the item had no intrinsic value. That made it difficult for Harriet to know which collectibles scattered around the immense house were valuable and which ones had simply struck Grandad's fancy. Neither did she know which items he'd collected and which ones he'd inherited from his own parents. Or even his grandparents.

The Bailey family had been at Cobble Hill Farm since the house was built in 1820. A portrait of Harriet's great-great-grandfather hung on the landing of the stairs that led to the second floor. His name was Harold too, but, unlike Grandad, the first Harold appeared stony and cold in his portrait. None of Grandad's photographs showed him with an icy demeanor, and no one would ever describe Old Doc Bailey in any way but warm and good-humored.

Perhaps Harriet should take Harold's portrait to the festival for an expert opinion on its value. But unless the artist, a name Harriet didn't recognize, was famous, the frame was probably more valuable than the painting.

Aunt Jinny considered for a moment then said, "Take the umbrella stand. Dad hates it, but it was a gift from a friend."

Harriet smiled at how Aunt Jinny sometimes talked about her father in the present tense, as if he were still with them.

Looking around the entryway and into the adjoining reading nook, she couldn't help feeling that perhaps he was part of the crowd of witnesses mentioned by the writer of Hebrews. After all, this house was still much more Grandad's than hers with its dark woods and leather furnishings.

"The umbrella stand it is then," Harriet said. "I'll get a box."

A short time later, the golden stand with its floral design was safely stored next to a hideous gargoyle about the size of a shoebox in the trunk of Aunt Jinny's sporty red Renault Clio. The gargoyle had the eroded appearance of a chiseled stone that had been exposed to a century of inclement weather.

"Where did that come from?" Harriet asked.

Aunt Jinny's eyes sparkled as she closed the trunk, which she'd call the boot. "He was tucked away in a corner of the attic, but don't ask me how he got there or where he came from, because I don't have the answer to either of those questions. I went to the attic to see what treasures I could find, and he was there. And now he's here." She waved her hand in a dramatic gesture over the Renault's trunk. "I've named him Winston."

"Winston? After Churchill?"

"Who else? I think the former prime minister would be honored and amused."

"Do you think it's worth anything?" Harriet tried to keep the doubt from her voice but failed miserably.

Aunt Jinny's laugh was the warm hug Harriet needed to shoo away the unsettled ache surrounding her. She laughed too, though she couldn't say why, as she slid into the front passenger seat and fastened her seat belt, while congratulating herself for not accidentally sliding into the driver's seat. By the time she was able to visit her parents, she'd probably think their cars were the weird ones.

Aunt Jinny drove to the spacious public meadow that overlooked the pounding waves of the North Sea where community events were commonly held. Colorful banners and decorated tents dotted the grounds. Food booths vied for attention with carnival games. Calliope music from a few of the rides was periodically drowned out by the shouts of excited children. Other rides, such as the Ferris wheel, were in the final construction stages.

A large pavilion in the center of the meadow hosted the festival's main event—at least, its *intended* main event. Aunt Jinny explained that the interior had been transformed into a museum where all the antiques were displayed on shelves or in glass cabinets. The experts appraised the items on their own then selected certain ones to showcase. Though they scheduled time to talk to each owner about his or her contribution, only their conversations with the owners of the showcased antiques were filmed by a local video production company.

Harriet and Aunt Jinny carried their items to the pavilion, stopping several times along the way to greet friends and neighbors. Sometimes it seemed to Harriet that her aunt knew everyone in Yorkshire and had been present at the birth of many of them. Eventually, they reached the registration area, where Ivy Chapman reigned behind a waist-high counter on the veranda outside the pavilion's huge double doors.

"There you are, Dr. Garrett," Ivy said to Aunt Jinny. "I can't wait to see the worthy antique you brought for the appraisers. And this must be your niece, the American veterinarian I've heard so much about. My sister, Fern, said you worked miracles with that nasty old goat of hers. Why Fern keeps that aged animal is beyond me. I suspect it's mostly to spite me. She's so perverse. As soon as I advise her one way, she goes the other. I've never known the like from anyone else. Show me what you have, and I'll get you registered."

Harriet's eyes had widened with each new sentence that Ivy uttered without taking a breath. Even if Alma Wilkerson hadn't mentioned that Ivy and Fern were sisters, Harriet would have guessed they were closely related. Both women appeared to be in their mid-fifties and had auburn hair, striking green eyes, and slender figures.

Fern had said nothing about a sister when Harriet visited her small farm to tend to the pet goat a few weeks ago. In fact, Harriet was certain that Fern, who was as talkative as Ivy, had given the impression she was an only child whose parents had died several years before. She'd had a beau when she was young, but they'd quarreled, and she vowed never to give her heart away again. Fern had advised Harriet to make the same promise to herself.

Even though Harriet had recently experienced her own broken heart, she wasn't about to make that vow. Though, strange to say, she wasn't as sad about the end of her engagement as she'd been a few months ago. The death of her grandfather had overshadowed that loss, and the details of a permanent move from the United States to England had taken much of her attention. To her surprise, her heart was mending sooner than she'd thought possible.

The registration process didn't take long with Ivy in charge. She had much to say about Aunt Jinny's gargoyle—none of it flattering—but she gushed over the uniqueness of Harriet's umbrella stand.

They were given receipts for their items and a packet with information about the appraisal process and schedule.

"She called poor Winston ugly," Aunt Jinny said when they were out of earshot. She feigned offense then laughed as she led the way to the food booths. "It's a gargoyle. He's supposed to be ugly."

"I'm relieved she liked my umbrella stand." After hearing Ivy's critique of the gargoyle, Harriet had been hesitant to remove her item from its box. "She's going to be more disappointed than I will if it turns out to be from some big-box store."

"Not all of those are bad. I like several of them, actually." Aunt Jinny directed Harriet to the Biscuit Bistro booth and introduced her to Poppy Schofield, the fortyish woman behind the table. Harriet no longer needed to remind herself that a British biscuit was an American cookie.

She was trying to decide between a Cornish fairing, which was a spiced ginger biscuit perfect for autumn, or an Empire biscuit, a Scottish iced cookie with raspberry jam, when her aunt's conversation caught her attention.

"It's a mystery to be sure," Poppy was saying to Aunt Jinny. "And not only my store has been bothered. Mr. Calabash walked into his insurance agency one morning to find that all the pictures in his office had been moved around. Not a one where he usually had them."

"That sounds like a prank to me," Aunt Jinny replied. "Are you sure that incident is related to the theft at your store?"

"Only those responsible know," Poppy said. "I've talked to DC Worthington, and he agrees it's mighty mysterious for someone to break in and do such a thing. I wouldn't have minded so much if they'd taken the orange floral cookie jar, as it was never one of my favorites, but for a thief to take the coral rose one—that's simply unforgivable. I intended to bring it for the appraisal exhibit, and now I can't. The perpetrator must be found."

Harriet's heart pounded. Since she'd moved to the charming village of White Church Bay, she'd been embroiled in one mysterious adventure after another. She prayed Aunt Jinny was right, that Poppy's theft and Mr. Calabash's prank were typical small-town mischief.

But something in the air—and it wasn't the bracing wind from the sea—sent a shiver up her spine. So-called harmless pranks often weren't viewed that way by the victims. And if the same pranksters were also thieves, what might they decide to do next? Who would be their next target?

CHAPTER TWO

Harriet inwardly laughed at how she imagined herself as a super-powered crime fighter when she and Aunt Jinny purchased cookies and small bottles of water adorned with the Biscuit Bistro logo on the label. Harriet exchanged the proper money for a white paper bag containing both a Cornish fairing and an Empire biscuit, pleased that she no longer had to second-guess herself or even thought of the pounds and shillings as foreign currency. The silver and gold coins, even the seven-sided fifty-pence piece, were as familiar to her now as dollars and dimes.

"One of my patients told me a similar story," Aunt Jinny said as they meandered away from Poppy's booth. "She owns a fabric shop a couple doors down from the Biscuit Bistro. A week or so ago, she found a basket of notions had been moved from the counter to a shelf. A remnant of purple satin was draped around a mannequin, and a quilting project had been spread across the cutting table."

"How strange. Was anything taken?"

"She didn't think so, though of course any small items, such as spools of thread or buttons, could be missing and she wouldn't know without doing an inventory." Aunt Jinny sipped her water. "She'd suspected her teenage boys had snuck into the store since there was no sign of a break-in, but they denied it. They're a family of practical jokers, though, so she'd already come up with a way to retaliate and wanted my help."

"What did she want you to do?"

"She thought it'd be hilarious to tell them I'd diagnosed her with a debilitating disease that would leave her bedridden for the next fifty years and that she'd require their constant care."

Harriet couldn't imagine her aunt agreeing to such a cruel prank, but she still had much to learn about British humor. "What did you say?"

"Her boys are mischievous and high-spirited, but they're also kindhearted. I told her that too many people face horrific health concerns for such a prank to be funny. Hopefully she came up with a less devastating idea."

"What if her boys were telling the truth? If she plays a practical joke on them, won't they retaliate?"

"I'm sure they will. But eventually they'll all have a good laugh and everything will be fine." Aunt Jinny's brows drew together. "Unless they're the ones who broke into Poppy's shop and Mr. Calabash's insurance agency. Perhaps I should have a talk with them, especially now that the pranks have escalated to thievery."

"That's assuming that whoever took the coral rose cookie jar is the same person or persons who moved things around in the other stores," Harriet said. "Did Poppy say how the thief got into her store?"

"Come to think of it, she didn't. If her lock had been jimmied or a window broken, I think she would have mentioned it."

"It's our own locked-room mystery," Harriet said in an eerie voice, fluttering her fingers. "Maybe we should talk to Poppy again. And to Mr. Calabash and your friend."

Aunt Jinny looped her arm through Harriet's. "Or maybe we should enjoy the festival and leave any investigating to Detective Constable Worthington. He might appreciate the opportunity to solve a mystery without our help for once."

Aunt Jinny was probably right, but Harriet couldn't stop her imagination from conjuring up visions of mysterious apparitions unhindered by locks and doors. Not that she believed in ghosts. But she enjoyed what Anne Shirley once described as a "delicious fear" when she and Diana Berry took a shortcut through the Haunted Woods in *Anne of Green Gables*.

The two women made the circuit of the booths and attractions, stopping along the way for occasional chats with other festival-goers. Aunt Jinny introduced Harriet to villagers she hadn't yet met. Though she enjoyed meeting them, Harriet couldn't guarantee she'd remember all the names or this-person-is-related-to-that-person info being tossed at her.

She was surprised to find she was still something of a local celebrity—Old Doc Bailey's American granddaughter who'd taken over the veterinary practice and now lived at Cobble Hill Farm. The warm welcome pushed away the remnants of homesickness that had engulfed her earlier in the day. And all her imaginings about ghosts rearranging the cookie trays in the Biscuit Bistro.

Before long, Harriet and Aunt Jinny were back at the pavilion. Ivy wasn't at her post, but the double doors were open, so they went inside to find their items among the other antiques and collectibles on display for the experts to appraise and visitors to admire.

"Ivy can't be far away," Aunt Jinny murmured to Harriet. "She wants to register every item that comes in herself so there are no mix-ups or mishaps. I suppose that's understandable, given her role—"

Aunt Jinny broke off, and an amused smile rounded her cheeks. "There's your exquisite umbrella stand, placed where everyone can see it."

Harriet's contribution stood on top of a faux mantel along with other Asian-inspired objects.

"It does seem to be in a prominent place. Which will make it even more embarrassing when the expert tells me it was mass-produced." Harriet swept her gaze over the nearby displays. "Where's your gargoyle?"

Aunt Jinny waved her hand toward a far wall. "Tucked away in that corner. My beloved Winston didn't impress Ivy at all."

"Does she really make all these decisions on her own?"

"This is her show," Aunt Jinny said. "And we are merely players."

As they returned to the veranda, Fern Chapman rushed to the registration counter.

"Ivy is nowhere to be found," she exclaimed to the man and woman sitting there. "She's supposed to be on the main stage to make the announcements and introduce the school choir. The students are ready to perform, but Ivy has disappeared, and no one knows where to find her."

The man, his thick eyebrows furrowed, started to say something, but Fern didn't give him a chance.

"I knew it was a mistake to put her in charge of the events committee. I would never have shirked my duty by wandering off. But Ivy is so forgetful. I warned you and everyone else again and again, but no one listened to me."

Aunt Jinny touched Fern's arm. "I'm sure Ivy didn't wander off," she said. "It's not like her to do such a thing. Something important must have come up that needed her attention."

"What's more important than making sure our Antique Festival runs like clockwork?" Fern demanded. "Since Ivy isn't here to do her job, I'll have to pick up the slack. Just like I always do." She bustled toward the main stage.

"I don't think we can stop her," the man said. "But Ivy isn't going to like it."

"Then she should have been here," the woman beside him replied. She turned to greet someone else.

"Despite her protests," Aunt Jinny said in a quiet undertone to Harriet, "Fern loves the opportunity to be in the spotlight. She agreed to chair the setup and cleanup committee because it was the only slot still open by the time she made up her mind to volunteer. But it galls her that Ivy chairs the events committee every year."

"Is Fern right about Ivy?" Harriet asked. "Could she have forgotten about emceeing the show?"

"Not Ivy," Aunt Jinny said. "She's as sharp as they come."

As if in response, Fern's voice crackled over the loudspeakers set up around the stage. "Welcome, everyone. I'm Fern Chapman, though most of you already know that. But if you didn't, now you do." She gave a girlish giggle. "Thank you all for coming out today, and we hope you'll be back tomorrow and the next day, and all the other days of our festival. And bring your friends. We have lots of entertainment and food, and a brand-new dunk tank! I suppose you might want to check out our appraisals event, which really takes too much work, because—well, it isn't easy to find experts. Not that we don't have a lot of experts, but to find the best. And then the one we wanted most couldn't come, so we had to find a substitute, but—"

Aunt Jinny rolled her eyes. "This is why Ivy usually serves as the emcee."

"Maybe we should try to find her," Harriet suggested. "Any ideas on where to begin?"

"I imagine she'll come running now that she's heard Fern's voice," Aunt Jinny said with a chuckle. "But let me try calling her."

Aunt Jinny tapped her cell phone screen while leading the way to the main stage. After a moment she left a message then ended the call with a determined expression. "I believe I'll suggest to Fern that she make an announcement requesting Ivy to join her. Better yet, I'll make it myself."

Harriet stood by the corner of the stage, glad she wasn't the one who had to wrest the microphone from Fern's grasp. Aunt Jinny, with her usual poise and dignity, managed to do so without too much of a scene.

"Excuse me for a moment, folks," she said with a broad smile. "We're looking for Ivy Chapman. Ivy, if you can hear me, you're needed at the main stage." Aunt Jinny put a slight emphasis on the word *needed*. "Thanks, everyone." She waved at the crowd, handed the mic to Fern, and returned to Harriet.

The minutes passed slowly as Fern mangled a couple more announcements and introduced the choir, all the while furtively scanning the crowd. Was she on the lookout for Ivy, hoping she wouldn't show up and take the spotlight from her? She certainly didn't seem concerned about her sister's absence.

The third time Aunt Jinny called Ivy without getting an answer, Harriet nudged her. "Maybe we should search for her."

"Good idea. I'll go this way, you go that way, and we'll meet back here."

A few bystanders overheard the conversation and volunteered to help, so Aunt Jinny gave them directions as well. With so many people involved, Harriet was confident they would soon find the missing woman.

But when the group reconvened at the stage, where Fern mispronounced the name of the next student group to perform, Ivy was still nowhere to be found.

By this time, DC Van Worthington had joined the search. A handsome man in his midtwenties, he had a certain boyish charm. His eyes were hazel instead of puppy-dog brown, but they were especially spaniel-like whenever he was around Polly. Sadly for Van, Polly already had several young men vying for her attention.

Harriet had come to respect him and, even better, to like him. She eagerly supported his efforts to put together a formal search party.

When Fern finally left the stage, she appeared stunned to learn Ivy hadn't been found. "Perhaps she had a secret rendezvous," she suggested, a blush appearing on her powdered cheeks. "And forgot the time."

"That's highly unlikely," Aunt Jinny replied. "Besides, I've tried to call her several times, and she isn't answering."

Until then, it seemed that the group had expected Ivy to suddenly appear out of nowhere and chide them for making a fuss. But the consensus among those who knew Ivy best—all those except

Fern, who downplayed their concerns—was that she'd never leave such an important event of her own free will.

"She might have fallen somewhere," Van said as he glanced at the nearby woods. "Though we've checked all the likely spots around here."

"Perhaps she went home for a nap and slept through her alarm," someone suggested.

Mr. Calabash, a rotund, well-dressed Black Brit, said, "I checked her house. She wasn't there."

"I've never been one to break patient-doctor confidentiality," Aunt Jinny whispered to Harriet, "but say someone was on a new medication."

"And had a reaction?" Harriet asked, immediately aware of what her aunt was suggesting. "Perhaps she's unconscious. But where?"

"I wish we knew."

The sound of an engine drew their attention, and Van's worried expression eased as he hurried toward an orange SUV. "I called Skippy Stiles. He'll find Ivy for us."

"Who's Skippy Stiles?" Harriet asked.

Aunt Jinny rushed after Van. "Come on. I'll introduce you."

By the time they reached the mud-splattered vehicle, a man with a squat build and confident posture had emerged from the driver's side. He wore a tweed flat cap over close-cropped white hair and a hip-length jacket with an array of pockets. He opened the back hatch, and a sleek border collie jumped to the ground. The black fur on either side of the white blaze on the dog's nose was shot with gray. He politely sat on Skippy's left side, ears alert.

Skippy warmly greeted Van and Aunt Jinny then faced Harriet. "Who's this?"

"My niece, Harriet Bailey," Aunt Jinny said. "She took over Dad's practice. Harriet, this is Edward Stiles, better known around here as Skippy. He grew up locally but moved to Scotland to attend university and stayed. That's where his parents were from."

"So you're the American granddaughter," Skippy said with a warm smile. "Old Doc often talked about you. This is Jiffy." He patted the dog's neck.

"Your dog's name is Jiffy?" Harriet asked. "And you're called Skippy?"

He grinned. "My dear late wife, an American like yourself, insisted on naming him that because he was such a quick little pup. Always on the move."

"Jiffy is a search and rescue dog," Van explained. "He's known all over the country for tracking lost people."

"In his prime, he was the best," Skippy agreed. "We're semiretired now. That's why I'm here in Yorkshire, taking a bit of a holiday. We make it a point to visit the old stomping grounds whenever we can. Would you like to accompany me on this hunt for Ivy? See Jiffy in action?"

"Very much," Harriet replied. She'd always been fascinated by the work of SAR dogs.

"Jinny and Van, you come along too," Skippy said. "Fern, I know you're concerned about your sister, but would you stay and mind the crowd? Jiffy needs room to work, and we want to find Ivy as soon as possible."

Fern agreed as a myriad of expressions crossed her face—annoyance, dread, and frustration, to name a few. Harriet guessed she wanted to go with Jiffy but that she also enjoyed the concerned attention she was receiving from those crowding around her.

"Ivy would want the show to go on," she said in the tone of a film noir femme fatale. "We must keep our visitors entertained."

Fern went to Ivy's car and retrieved a sweater for Jiffy to catch Ivy's scent. Skippy and Jiffy then began their search at the counter where Ivy had registered the antiques. Within moments, Jiffy started off across the grounds followed by Skippy, Aunt Jinny, Van, and Harriet. A couple of times he paused and sniffed around for a while, but then he picked up the scent again, which took him to the edge of the meadow.

To Harriet's surprise, Jiffy trotted to the edge of the cliff overlooking the sea. None of the searchers had checked there because, as far as they knew, Ivy had no reason to go there.

The ground was flat with no trees or boulders to block their view. Beyond the cliff edge, the rising and falling waves of the North Sea stretched toward the horizon and met the eastern sky. Even if Ivy had tripped and fallen, they should be able to see her. Unless she'd fallen over—

Harriet refused to finish the thought even as Jiffy stood at the edge of the cliff and peered back at them. "I've never been this way before," she said. "It looks dangerous."

"There's a path that leads to the beach," Aunt Jinny assured her, though anxiety colored her tone. "It's a bit treacherous. Rocks just far enough into the sea that one can't even get to the village from here. I have no idea why Ivy would come this way."

"Maybe Fern was right about a secret rendezvous," Harriet said, holding out hope that they'd find Ivy strolling along the shore instead of sprawled on the stones beneath the cliff.

When they reached Jiffy, Skippy and Van were the first to peer over. "She's not down there," Van said, relief in his voice. "At least, I don't see her."

"Then we take the path," Skippy replied. "Walk on, Jiff, my boy." The border collie replied with a resounding bark. He wagged his tail then disappeared from Harriet's view as he trotted along the path to the shore. She stepped closer to the path, intent on watching Jiffy.

"You ladies should stay here," Van said. "Skippy and I will follow the path and let you know if we find her."

"Ivy may need medical attention," Aunt Jinny protested. "Besides, I've used this path hundreds of times."

"I'm going too," Harriet insisted. Despite her fear of navigating the treacherous path, there was no way she would let the others leave her behind.

"Okay then." Skippy obviously preferred not to waste time arguing. "I'll go first. Van, you bring up the rear."

The packed-dirt path seemed to have been cut out of the side of the cliff itself. The long and narrow slope required all Harriet's inner strength to convince herself she could follow it to the bottom without stumbling. Provided she didn't stub her toe on any of the rocks that poked out of the dirt as if placed there to cause a fall.

Oh great. First I'm fantasizing about ghosts going through doors to play pranks and steal things, and now I'm getting paranoid.

Not at all like her usual, practical "ghosts don't exist" self. Though how practical had it been to uproot her entire life, leave her parents and lifelong friends behind, and sail across an ocean? Not practical at all, but Mom had praised her courage while Dad had encouraged her to embrace his ancestral roots. Maybe something about the Yorkshire air caused her thoughts to turn more fanciful.

And maybe she was trying to avoid thinking about what she feared to find at the bottom of the path.

They called Ivy's name over and over, but there was no response. Aunt Jinny's frequent phone calls remained unanswered. From all accounts, Ivy was devoted to the Antique Festival, particularly the appraisals, and thrived on being the emcee. So what was keeping her from her duties?

Jiffy waited for them at the bottom of the path then trotted close to the cliff as tidal waves encroached on the slender beach.

"He's going into the cave," Van exclaimed.

Aunt Jinny's eyes widened. "I believe you're right. Why would Ivy go in there?"

They jogged after Jiffy. "What cave?" Harriet shouted to make her voice heard above the roaring waves.

"It's said to be a pirates' lair. And centuries before that, a Viking hideout." Aunt Jinny pointed to a dark shadow in the cliff wall. "There it is."

Jiffy disappeared into the shadow while Skippy beckoned the rest of them to catch up. "The sea flows into the cave, but there's room to walk on either side of the stream." He pulled a small flashlight from one of the many pockets in his jacket. "I have a wee torch. Anyone else have one?"

"I do," Van said, brandishing his own flashlight.

"We can use our phones," Harriet said to Aunt Jinny.

As they turned on their flashlight apps, a menacing bark sounded from the depths of the cave followed by a yelp of pain, then silence.

"Jiffy," Skippy cried.

Everyone followed him as he rushed into the cave, splashing through the channel of water and waving his flashlight beam from one side of the cave to the other.

Until the light fell upon two prone bodies lying against the cave wall.

Ivy sprawled on her back, a trail of blood streaking from her temple and along her cheek. Jiffy lay on his side next to her.

Van aimed his stronger beam toward the rear of the cave. It extended beyond the light, but nothing moved in the shadows. All was still.

Deathly still.

CHAPTER THREE

Aunt Jinny crouched beside Ivy while Harriet tended to Jiffy. "She's breathing," Aunt Jinny assured them while she conducted a quick assessment for injuries.

Van shone his flashlight on the unconscious woman's face. Ivy moaned and stirred but didn't open her eyes.

"I'll contact emergency services." Van spoke into his radio, but the signal must have been blocked by the surrounding rock, because he hurried to the entrance of the cave.

Harriet ran her hands over the border collie's fur. "Jiffy doesn't appear to have any broken bones," she said. "We should move him to give Aunt Jinny more room."

"Aye," Skippy said, handing Harriet his flashlight. "We can do that." With a grunt, he heaved Jiffy into his arms. He cradled the dog and sloshed through the water toward the opening.

"How can I help you?" Harriet asked her aunt, who was dabbing water from her Biscuit Bistro bottle onto Ivy's face.

"By taking care of Jiffy. He needs you."

Harriet put her hand on Aunt Jinny's arm. "He does. But Ivy comes first."

As if she'd heard her name, Ivy stirred again, and her eyelids fluttered. "'Twas the ghost," she muttered. "Come from the dark."

Harriet and Aunt Jinny stared at each other.

"Ivy?" Aunt Jinny said, her voice firm. "Wake up, Ivy."

"I…am awake." Her eyes opened, and she focused her gaze on Aunt Jinny. "Where are we?"

"In the old pirate cave," Aunt Jinny said. "What happened?"

Ivy's eyes widened, and her voice strengthened. "The dog. 'Twas Jiffy, wasn't it? That fiend hit him."

"Who did?" Harriet asked.

Ivy directed her gaze toward Harriet. "You're Doc Bailey's granddaughter. The American vet."

"That's right. I'm Harriet. We met earlier, remember?"

Ivy's expression shifted from confusion to fear. "You won't believe me. No one will believe me."

"Tell us what you saw," Aunt Jinny said in her no-nonsense tone, one that Harriet remembered from childhood visits when she and her cousin, Anthony, got into mischief.

When Ivy still hesitated, Aunt Jinny's tone softened. "We need to know who did this to you, Ivy. I've been your doctor since I opened my practice. You'd returned from university, and you were trying to decide which job offer to accept. Remember?"

"I turned them all down," Ivy said. "I missed White Church Bay too much while I was away to leave it for good."

"That's right." Aunt Jinny smiled as she folded her scarf to create a compress. She poured water on it and placed it against Ivy's forehead. "You trusted me to help you then. Trust me now."

Ivy's hands twitched, and Harriet took them in her own. The gesture seemed to help Ivy focus. "I saw King Arthur's knight. Ghostly, he was. He hit me, and when Jiffy tried to protect me, he hit

Jiffy." Tears sparkled in her eyes as she peered around the cave. "Where is that brave dog?"

"Skippy carried him outside," Harriet assured her while her mind raced with questions. Aunt Jinny had hinted that Ivy could experience strange side effects from a new prescription. But her injuries certainly hadn't been caused by a hallucinated medieval ghost. "You need to lie still so Aunt Jinny can tend to you."

"Which she's doing." Ivy's grip strengthened as she squeezed Harriet's fingers. "Now you need to do your job and tend to Jiffy. Please."

Harriet glanced at Aunt Jinny, who nodded. "Send Van in. We'll be fine."

Ivy tried to sit up, and Aunt Jinny gently pressed her back. "You stay still," she ordered.

"I'm not an invalid," Ivy protested.

"No one said you were." Aunt Jinny's no-nonsense tone had returned. "But you may have a concussion, so you'll stay put until your doctor says otherwise."

Harriet didn't stay to hear the end of the argument. After all, she had no doubt that Aunt Jinny would emerge the victor. Doing her best to ignore her wet legs, she sloshed through the center channel as Skippy had done, which was quicker than trudging the side paths next to the cave's rock walls.

As she neared the exit, she saw Skippy kneeling on the beach beside his border collie.

Van finished talking on his radio nearby as she approached. "Medical services are on the way," he told her. "They'll be here soon."

"That's good. Ivy's conscious." Harriet passed along Aunt Jinny's request that Van join her in the cave, and he immediately disappeared into the dark shadows. Harriet knelt at Jiffy's head and ran her hands along his neck to get him used to her touch. He emitted a low moan, but his eyes remained closed.

"How is he?"

"He's breathing," Skippy said, his voice gruff with emotion. "Someone walloped him upside the head. No need for anyone to do that to old Jiff, nor to Ivy."

"I agree with you there." Harriet examined the gash between Jiffy's ears. Skippy had used an oversize bandanna to stop the bleeding, but the wound needed to be cleaned and maybe stitched. She studied the sloping path that led to the top of the cliff. Coming down that path hadn't been as difficult as she'd feared. But she couldn't imagine how they could climb back up safely while carrying Jiffy. "We need to get him to the clinic."

"I already made the arrangements." Skippy stared at the sky. "Here they come now."

Harriet followed his gaze as a dark speck appeared against a white cloud. As it came closer, the *whomp-whomp* of the blades grew louder.

"Have you ever ridden in a search and rescue helicopter?" he asked.

"Can't say that I have."

"It'll be a short trip," Skippy explained. "They'll take us to the car park then transport Ivy to a hospital in Whitby." *Car park* was a British term for a parking lot or garage.

"I'm not sure Ivy will be happy about that," Harriet said as she returned to examining Jiffy. She wasn't sure she was either. The last thing she'd expected when she woke up that morning was an emergency ride in a helicopter. But she hadn't expected to follow a border collie into a deep, dark seaside cave once inhabited by Vikings and pirates either.

"She'll be irritated," Skippy said. "But a blow to the head is nothing to take lightly. The DC agreed with me."

"So do I." Especially after hearing Ivy's mysterious claim that her assailant had been a knight from King Arthur's court. Like many Americans, Harriet knew the basic story about the famous king and Guinevere, his queen. He'd specifically designed Camelot's round table so that no knight had a place of honor above any other knight. But that was about the extent of her knowledge.

Even though Harriet couldn't believe Ivy's medieval ghost story, the woman's wounds and Jiffy's proved that someone—a living, breathing someone—had attacked them.

Harriet traced the hairs on Jiffy's graying muzzle. "Such a sweet boy," she murmured as she raised his lips to check the color of his gums. She saw something dark caught in his teeth. "What's this?" She removed the frayed scrap of scarlet fabric, careful to touch only a soggy edge with her forefinger and thumb.

"He must have torn that from the assailant," Skippy said. He pulled a plastic bag from one of his many pockets. "It's evidence. Put it in here."

Harriet slid the scrap into the bag then smoothed it and examined the fabric. An embroidered design in gold thread decorated one edge of the irregular triangle. The threads of the remaining edges were frayed where Jiffy had torn the scrap from—what? A ghost knight's clothing?

No, not a ghost knight. The scrap had come from whatever Ivy's assailant was wearing.

A spine-tingling finger of anxious excitement zipped through her. Another mystery needed to be solved, and she was determined to solve it.

"It's not only evidence," she said to Skippy. "It's a clue."

The rescue helicopter arrived, making further conversation impossible. It hovered above them, the large blades stirring the grasses on top of the cliff and the sand on the beach. Two medics dressed in flight gear descended in a cage-like structure.

Van, who must have heard the commotion, came out to greet them. After a quick discussion, one man followed him into the cave with a stretcher and a duffel bag. The other hurried to Harriet and Skippy and knelt in front of Jiffy.

"What happened to him?" he asked.

"Don't know." Skippy nodded toward Harriet. "She's the new vet. Took over for Old Doc Bailey. We need to get him to her clinic."

"Right away."

Harriet's pulse quickened, and her eyes rounded as she stared at the helicopter. Perhaps she could hike back up the trail to the cliff top while they were getting Ivy on board.

Skippy laid a comforting hand on her arm. "I know what you're thinking, but there's no time to lose. Jiffy and I've been pulled up dozens of times. I promise, it's perfectly safe."

Reason told her she couldn't expect the helicopter to wait for her to trek up the trail. And Skippy was right. Jiffy needed her attention as soon as possible. She took a deep breath. "Being suspended in a cage in midair wasn't on my bucket list, but I guess I can cross it off anyway," she joked.

The medic smiled at her. "Go on with Skippy then. I've got Jiffy."

Skippy hesitated, and Harriet sensed he didn't want to leave Jiffy to someone else's care. But she'd also noticed how he'd struggled to carry the dog from the cave.

"Now it's my turn to know what *you're* thinking," she said quietly, tugging him to his feet as she stood. "You did your job in finding Ivy. Now it's time to let the rescue team do theirs."

Skippy grunted and stood aside while the medic lifted the border collie. They stepped into the cage, the three humans sitting in corners while Jiffy lay on a blanket between them. As soon as they were harnessed in, the medic signaled to the pilot, and the cage slowly rose toward the helicopter's open doors.

Though fear sat like a rock in Harriet's stomach, she also found the upward trip exhilarating. The festival grounds with its booths and carnival rides shrank into a collage of colors, and the distant woods resembled a child's toy forest.

In less time than she'd have thought possible, the cage was inside the helicopter's belly. A crew member handed her a headset with huge protective earpads and assisted her to her seat. She fastened her harness and seat belt while Skippy insisted on sitting on the floor with Jiffy sprawled across his lap. They were soon joined by Ivy, strapped to the stretcher, and Aunt Jinny, who took the seat beside Harriet.

A few minutes later, the helicopter landed at Cobble Hill Farm in the open space between the kennels and the art gallery. Harriet breathed a sigh of relief that they didn't have to be lowered in the cage. Once she was on solid ground, her legs needed a moment to stop wobbling.

The medic put his hand on her shoulder and shouted in her ear, "Where do we take Jiffy?"

"This way," she shouted back. She waited for him to lift Jiffy then hurried toward the clinic with the medic and Skippy following her.

As soon as Jiffy was settled on the surgical table, the medic raced away. The roar of the helicopter faded while Harriet scrubbed her hands. As she examined Jiffy's wound, Skippy collapsed into a nearby chair. She kept a wary eye on him as she administered an anesthetic to the collie. Maybe Skippy should have gone to the hospital with Aunt Jinny and Ivy.

"Do you need a drink? We keep a few bottles of water in the fridge over there."

"I'll be all right as soon as I know Jiffy is." He clenched his tweed cap in one beefy hand. "We've never had anything like this happen before. The people we find often have a few injuries. Hypothermia a couple of times. Dehydration too. Jiffy once got so many brambles caught in his coat that we had to shave him to treat all the scratches."

"Goodness," Harriet murmured as she worked.

Skippy turned away. "He was so embarrassed. As if he knew he wasn't his usual handsome self. Maybe you don't believe that's possible, for a dog to be embarrassed."

"I know it is," Harriet assured him while she cleaned and stitched the wound. Intelligent animals like border collies experienced more emotions than most people realized. She didn't doubt Skippy's story in the slightest. "Hopefully that fabric scrap can lead us to his attacker."

Skippy's eyes widened. "Us?"

"I mean the police."

"Well, it's in their hands now. I gave the scrap to the crew chief. He'll see the DC gets it."

That must have happened in the helicopter while Harriet sat strapped in her seat with her eyes closed. If only she'd been able to take another look at the fabric. Or better yet, had taken a photo.

She cut the thread and applied a bandage. "All done," she said to Skippy as she tossed her latex gloves in the dustbin. "He'll need to stay here for a few hours so I can keep an eye on his recovery."

"Thank ye, lass." Skippy swiped his hand over his eyes. "I know his time's coming sooner than I want, but it doesn't need to be today."

"It won't be. I have nothing else to do but watch over him."

The two of them worked together to move the sedated Jiffy into a post-op kennel. Skippy stood beside the open cage door while he cupped Jiffy's paw in his hand. "I don't like leaving him. Mind if I stick around for a bit?"

"Stay as long as you wish. I'll make us a cup of tea." One thing Harriet had learned during her few months in England was that tea didn't cure all ills, but it sure helped soothe the spirit. "I'll be back soon."

As she crossed the threshold from the clinic to the kitchen, Maxwell scampered toward her. She greeted him with a quick cuddle and gave him a treat. He followed her to the sink, his large brown eyes watching her movements as she filled the kettle and arranged the tea things on a wooden tray.

"Let's see what else we can offer Skippy," she said to Maxwell, who yipped a joyful bark in response. Harriet chuckled as she opened a large tin to see what goodies were inside. Her cookie stash was running low, so her choice was shortbread rounds and chocolate digestives. She decided to serve both and arranged them on a plate.

The kettle whistled at the same moment her cell phone rang with a call from Aunt Jinny.

Harriet switched off the gas under the kettle and answered her phone. She put the call on speaker so she could talk and pour the hot water into the teapot at the same time.

After her initial greeting, Aunt Jinny asked about Jiffy then gave Harriet an update on Ivy. "She's unhappy we brought her here. 'A lot of fuss and bother about nothing,' she said. But the casualty department doctor insisted on admitting her for an overnight stay. I concurred with that decision."

Harriet mentally translated *casualty department* to ER. Another synonym, she'd learned, was A&E for accidents and emergencies.

"I'm sure it's for the best," she said. "Did Ivy say any more about what happened?"

"She won't say anything at all. She refuses to give any description to the hospital staff or to Van. I told him what she told us in the cave, but he stared at me like I was crazy."

"I think Ivy was right," Harriet said. "Not that she saw a medieval ghost, but that she saw someone dressed up like a knight. I found a scrap of material in Jiffy's mouth. Though I suppose that doesn't mean anything. It could have been from any old shirt or jacket, except there was gold embroidery on one edge in a boxy pattern. Does that make sense?"

"I think so," Aunt Jinny replied. "What did you do with it?"

"Skippy sealed it in an evidence bag, which he gave to the crew chief to give to Van," Harriet said. "If I'd known he was going to do that, I'd have taken a photo. I wonder if it's too late."

"Van will never let you take a photo now." Concern sounded in Aunt Jinny's voice. "It's his job to locate this ghost knight, Harriet. Not yours. Whoever hurt Ivy and Jiffy won't want to be found."

"But he needs to be caught before he can hurt anyone else."

"Not by you."

Aunt Jinny was right, of course. But her words, meant to dissuade Harriet from pursuing the assailant, instead summoned her stubborn streak. Dad had once compared Harriet and her tenacity to a dog with a bone. No matter the wisdom of Aunt Jinny's admonition, Harriet couldn't let go of the mystery.

"I know you're curious," Aunt Jinny said, apparently reading Harriet's mind. "Mysteries bring out the sleuth in both of us. But this is a matter best left to the authorities. We've done everything we can, both for Ivy and Jiffy. I'd say God put us in the right place at the right time, wouldn't you? Who better than a physician and a veterinarian to have found them?"

"True. I'm glad we were there."

"Then let's be satisfied with that."

Judging from Aunt Jinny's tone, she expected Harriet's assurance that she would be. Instead, Harriet changed the subject. "When will you be home? Should I come pick you up?"

"I want to stay here until Fern arrives. Though who knows when that will be? She's taken over the appraisal registrations even though other volunteers were there to do it. That's another reason Ivy is giving us so much trouble about staying the night at the hospital. She doesn't trust Fern to organize things properly, not that I can blame her for that. But I told her that even if she leaves the hospital, she can't return to the Antique Festival. At least not today."

Harriet covered the teapot with a crocheted cozy and added napkins to the tray. She didn't understand Fern. Even though Harriet didn't have any siblings, she was certain she'd be at the hospital with one who'd been brutally attacked. That was what sisters should do for each other, not engage in jealous rivalries.

"When you're ready to leave, let me know," Harriet said to her aunt. "I'll come get you. Don't worry about your car. We'll pick it up later."

"Thank you. And Harriet?"

"Yes?"

"Mind what I said. No sleuthing."

Harriet smiled at the phone as the call ended. "Did you hear that, Maxwell? I guess we'll enjoy tea instead."

She picked up the tray and headed for the clinic, Maxwell following behind. "What's Charlie up to?" she asked him, realizing she hadn't seen the cat since their hectic arrival. She wasn't surprised though. No doubt the earsplitting noise of the helicopter had frightened Charlie. She'd come out when she was ready.

As Harriet pushed through the door separating the house from the clinic, Skippy rushed toward her. "Jiffy's seizing up. His entire body." Without saying any more, he hurried back to the recovery area. Harriet set the tea tray on a nearby table and rushed behind him.

Jiffy lay there, stiff, as if he was paralyzed. Then his entire body shook uncontrollably.

Harriet immediately grabbed a vial and injected the medication into the loose skin at Jiffy's shoulder.

"What's happening to him?" Skippy demanded. "Is he dying?"

"Not if I can help it," Harriet muttered. She retrieved the oxygen cup she'd used when stitching Jiffy's wound and placed it on his muzzle. Perhaps the blow to his head had been more severe than she'd thought.

"We should do a CT scan," she told Skippy. "As a precaution."

"Whatever you think best," he said, his usual stoicism completely obliterated by his concern for his dog. "He's not simply a pet, you know. We're partners, Jiffy and me."

"I know." Harriet placed her hand on his arm. "I promise you he'll get the best care possible. And I'll make it my mission to find who did this to him."

No matter what Aunt Jinny said, Harriet would see justice done, both for Ivy and Jiffy.

CHAPTER FOUR

Harriet offered a brief prayer of thanks that she had a CT machine at the clinic so that they didn't have to transport Jiffy to the emergency clinic in Whitby. The trip itself might have worsened his condition. Once the test was complete, she evaluated the scan with Skippy peering over her shoulder.

"I see a slight contusion here." She pointed to the bone near Jiffy's right ear, close to where he'd been wounded.

"The attacker must have hit him with something hard," Skippy said, his tone a mixture of horror and disgust.

"At least there doesn't appear to be any internal swelling. Still, I'd like to keep him overnight in case he has any more seizures."

Skippy averted his gaze and cleared his throat. "Don't suppose you'd let an old man camp out on the floor next to him? I've slept in rougher conditions."

"It's not a practice I encourage." But how could Harriet refuse him when he looked so forlorn? "Though I don't suppose you can go anywhere when your car is still at the festival grounds. So is Aunt Jinny's."

"That is a hiccup, since one of us needs to stay with Jiffy. Maybe the DC can help us get the vehicles from there to here." Skippy pulled a phone from his pocket. "I'll call him and see."

"That's a great idea, but if he can't, we'll work something out tomorrow." Though if Van came to the clinic, Harriet could ask him about the fabric scrap. Maybe even talk him into giving her another chance to examine it. "While you do that, I'll get a place set up for you to camp out next to Jiffy. I think there's a cot in the attic."

Skippy's eyes brightened. "I can't thank you enough. And if Jiffy could talk, he'd say the same."

"I'm sure he'll rest better knowing you're near."

"I know I will. Don't think I'd sleep a wink if he wasn't close by."

Harriet gave him a smile then left him to make his call to the detective constable. As she passed the table where she'd left the tea tray, she rested her fingers against the rounded pot. The water had cooled too much to make a steaming cup of tea. She carried the tray into the kitchen, poured the water back into the kettle, and put it on the stove to reheat.

While she was climbing the attic stairs for the cot, her cell phone rang. She smiled at the photo that appeared on her screen.

Fitzwilliam "Will" Knight, the pastor of the village church, had posed for the snapshot several weeks ago when they'd eaten lunch together at Cliffside Chippy, a fish and chips takeout place on the bluff overlooking White Church Bay. It had been a surprisingly hot afternoon, or at least the local residents seemed to think so as they used whatever was handy to fan themselves.

Harriet had appreciated the warmth, and she'd been dazzled by the view of the sea as she and Will sat across from each other at a patio table.

Now she settled on a step and answered the phone with a cheery greeting.

"I heard you've had an adventurous afternoon." Will's voice, though as cheerful as Harriet's, held an undertone of concern that eased the underlying tension knotting her stomach. She appreciated Will's easygoing friendship, even if her heart remained bruised from her broken engagement and she wasn't at all ready for a new romance. He cared, and his caring gave her a peace that seemed to come straight from God.

"An adventure I would happily have given up for a leisurely stroll around the festival and having an expert tell me that my umbrella stand is worthless."

"You're fine though? No cuts or scratches?"

"None that I know about. Only Ivy and Jiffy were injured." Harriet gave him the details.

Not surprisingly, Will was already acquainted with Skippy and Jiffy from their previous holidays in White Church Bay. "Jiffy's a good dog. I hope he recovers soon," Will said. "I'm going to the hospital to see Ivy later. Would you like to go with me?"

"I wish I could, but Skippy thinks he'll be more comfortable on a cot in the clinic than in his own house without Jiffy."

"That's probably true. How can I help?"

Harriet grinned to herself, appreciating how he'd phrased the question. Not the typical *what can I do* but *how can I help*, as if his assistance was a given. A subtle difference, but an important one. Especially when she so often fought against the unhealthy mindset that she had to do everything herself. The mindset had embedded itself even deeper in her psyche when her dreams of the future had shattered at her feet. If she couldn't trust and depend on the man who was supposed to love her, how could she trust or depend on anyone else?

And yet she'd never have made it across the ocean without the loving, patient assistance of her parents, and she wouldn't have settled so quickly into her new home without the kindness of her aunt and others who'd welcomed her with their warm hospitality.

Will was one of those people, and while a pastor was expected to be friendly, Harriet considered him a friend every bit as much as her spiritual adviser. Especially considering the adventures they'd already shared in the few months she'd known him.

"Help me find who did this," she said in answer to his question.

Will chuckled. "I doubt Van wants our help. I get the impression he thinks you interfere too much in his cases as it is."

"But he's grateful for my input once the mystery is solved. Besides, I promised Skippy. If Jiffy takes a turn for the worse…" Her throat caught, choking off the rest of her sentence. In her professional opinion, Jiffy simply needed rest, antibiotics, and pain meds to aid in his healing from his injuries. But head wounds were seldom predictable. Skippy, who'd already lost his wife, didn't need to lose his dog too.

"He won't. Not when he has you as his vet," Will assured her. "Would you mind if I dropped by for a few minutes before I go to Whitby? I could pray with Skippy, and you can tell me about this ghost knight everyone is whispering about."

Harriet gasped in astonishment. "How do people already know about that?"

"So it's true?" Will asked in mock seriousness.

"Obviously the attacker wasn't a ghost." The kettle whistled again, and Harriet returned to the kitchen. The cot would have to wait a few more minutes. "Please come. We'll be in the clinic."

"I'm on my way."

By the time Will arrived, Harriet had the cot set up near Jiffy's kennel and persuaded Skippy to drink a cup of tea. He'd even eaten one of the chocolate digestives. He'd left a voice mail message for Van, so he didn't have any updates to provide.

Harriet left Skippy and Will with Jiffy, giving as her excuse that she wanted to find Charlie. She wasn't exactly worried about the cat, who had a remarkable knack for taking care of herself. But after what had happened to Jiffy, she felt the need to check on her. Plus, she sensed Skippy might appreciate the opportunity for a private visit with the local pastor.

After checking Charlie's favorite spots, Harriet finally found her lounging on the woodpile stacked against the back of the barn. The cat gave a leisurely stretch then relaxed when Harriet took her in her arms. Charlie's warmth and soft purrs were a tonic, and Harriet rested her cheek against the muted colors of the patchy tan, gray, and cream coat.

"Did that helicopter frighten you?" she asked softly. "It scared me, but the ride wasn't all that bad. It's amazing what you can do when you don't have a choice."

As she rounded the barn on her way back to the clinic, she saw Will on the patio holding two glasses of orange squash, a drink made with fruit-flavored syrup and water. He scanned the area, no doubt for her. She called to him, and he responded with a warm smile.

"Skippy refuses to leave Jiffy's side," he said when she joined him. "But I thought it might be nice for us to sit out here for a while. I still want to hear what you know about Ivy's ghost knight."

They settled in cushioned wicker chairs, their beverages on a table between them, in the landscaped area bordered by the house and clinic, the barn and kennels, and the art gallery. Charlie languished in Harriet's lap while Maxwell raced to greet Will. The dachshund placed his front paws on Will's legs and yipped in a plea to be held.

"Do you mind?" Will asked Harriet.

"Please. I imagine he can use the break."

Will released Maxwell from the wheelchair, a task he'd performed more than once before, and laid the dog across his legs. Maxwell released a contented sigh and closed his eyes.

Harriet took a long sip of the refreshing orange drink, smiling to herself that Will had remembered to add ice cubes to her glass. It was an American habit that ran counter to British custom.

With her two pets contentedly napping and the gusts of wind from the nearby North Sea blocked by the surrounding structures, Harriet breathed deeply of the salt-tinged air mingling with the various scents of color-changing leaves and autumn flowers. She cherished tranquil moments like this one and closed her eyes as she tucked it into her memory.

Several moments passed, and then she opened her eyes and slanted her gaze toward Will. He appeared lost in his own reverie as he rested a hand on Maxwell's round body. As if sensing Harriet's gaze, he turned to her.

"Tough day?" he teased.

"Unusual, that's for sure."

"Tell me."

As if the story had been a shaken soda bottle about to explode, she poured it out in a torrent of words, pausing only to answer an occasional question.

"I hadn't met Ivy before today, but everyone at the festival seemed concerned about her." Harriet frowned. "Except for Fern. But she couldn't have been the attacker. She was too busy taking over the emcee role."

"It's strange that anyone would want to hurt Ivy," Will said. "What was she doing in the cave?"

"No idea. Maybe Aunt Jinny will find out. Or Van." Harriet's mouth quirked with mischief. "Though he might not tell me if he did."

"He might as well," Will said, chuckling. "I can tell from the gleam in your eye that you're not about to sit aside while our conscientious DC solves this mystery."

Harriet grew serious. "I promised Skippy. Whoever did this to Ivy and Jiffy must be brought to justice."

"The mystery ghost soldier." Will shook his head. "How do we find a ghost?"

Harriet thought back to Ivy's words. "Not a soldier. Ivy said he was King Arthur's knight."

Will shifted in his seat while balancing Maxwell's long body. "Did she mean the lost drummer boy?"

"I don't know. Who's that?"

"An old legend that's famous around these parts." He glanced at his watch. "I should be leaving soon, so I'll give you the short version."

Harriet listened intently as Will told her about a little boy who was allegedly trapped in a narrow tunnel two or three centuries before. He'd been playing his drum so that the soldiers who were aboveground could follow his underground path and discover where the tunnel ended.

"The story goes that the drumming stops because the little boy discovers King Arthur and his knights sound asleep in a lighted cavern. One of the knights wakes up." Will opened his eyes wide to mimic the waking knight. "'Is England under attack?' the knight asks. When the boy assures him that England is safe, the knight says, 'Then it isn't time to awaken King Arthur. Will you stay with us until that time comes?' The boy says yes, and he's never seen again."

"I'm not sure whether to find that story disturbing or enchanting," Harriet said.

"I suppose it was meant to be comforting." Will cradled Maxwell and rose from his chair. The dachshund opened his eyes and licked Will's chin as Will reattached the prosthetic wheelchair to Maxwell's hind legs. "The legend changes a tragedy into a heroic story. From what I recall, the soldiers who sent the boy into the tunnel were horrified when the drumming stopped."

"Couldn't they dig him out?"

"They were too afraid. One version of the legend says that the boy had been eaten by a monster. They didn't want to free the monster from his underground lair."

"You're kidding."

"Whether or not that was their reason, I don't know. But it's part of the story."

Despite the sun's warmth, Harriet shivered. "Do you think the legend is a clue to the attacks? Not that I can see how it could be."

"I don't either, especially since the tunnel in the legend is in North Yorkshire." Will fastened the final strap on Maxwell's wheelchair then stood. "I haven't been there since I was young, but there's a walking trail and a stone that marks the place where the drumming stopped. A drummer boy statue too."

A familiar feeling surged through Harriet and quickened her pulse. The feeling that said, *this is important*.

"How do you feel about going there again?" she asked.

Will raised an eyebrow at her. "Richmond is over an hour away. Closer to an hour and a half."

Harriet had been in Yorkshire long enough to know that a three-hour round trip in one day, which wasn't a big deal to someone who lived in the States, seemed a Herculean task in England. "I'll drive," she offered. "It'll be fun. And we might learn something important."

Will's doubt eased into a reluctant smile. "I'll go with you. But I'll be the one driving."

"You doubt my ability to stay on the left side of the road for that long?"

"You doubt my ability not to hit a deer?"

Harriet gave him a sympathetic smile. He'd done exactly that a few weeks before. The incident totaled his vehicle, a former funeral hearse. Will now zipped along the Yorkshire lanes in a Kia Picanto, a tiny four-door hatchback. Harriet found it a much more suitable choice for a pastor.

"Okay." Harriet stood and placed Charlie in the chair. The cat meowed in protest then curled her tail around her body and closed her eyes. "You drive, and I'll buy lunch."

"My parents once took us to a little café that had pictures on the walls of medieval reenactors. I'll call Mum and see if she remembers the name of it."

"That sounds perfect. When can we go?"

"Sunday after church?"

"I suppose that's the best day for me too." Even when the clinic was closed, the veterinarian was always on duty. But Sundays did seem to be quieter than any other day of the week, and she could ask a colleague to cover any emergencies.

Harriet walked Will to his car and waved as he drove away. He'd arranged with Aunt Jinny to pick up her car after his visit with Ivy so that Harriet didn't need to go get her. Skippy still needed to retrieve his car, but that could wait until tomorrow if Van wasn't available this evening.

As she returned to the clinic, Harriet's thoughts were consumed with the legend of the lost drummer boy. Will's words about the story bringing comfort burrowed into her heart. Though she'd never been a mother, she couldn't imagine the heartache of losing a child in such a tragic way. But perhaps Will was right. That long-ago mother's little boy was still remembered to this day thanks to the legend.

And maybe, just maybe, that long-lost drummer boy held the key to unlock the mystery of the ghost knight in the cave.

CHAPTER FIVE

Wednesday morning passed quickly, even though each appointment took longer than normal thanks to Harriet's sudden celebrity status. Every client wanted to hear her firsthand account of finding Ivy and Jiffy in the cave and about her ride in the rescue helicopter. Embarrassed by the attention, Harriet did her best to downplay her role in the adventure and keep the focus on her work, but with limited success.

Last night, when Van returned Skippy's call, he said that he'd gone back to the cave to look for evidence and another way in or out of the tunnel. Then he'd driven to Whitby, first to drop off the scrap of fabric at the crime lab for processing and then to interview Ivy in the hospital. But if he'd found anything or uncovered any clues, he kept that information to himself.

According to Aunt Jinny, who'd visited Harriet after Will brought her home, Ivy had been less than forthcoming when it came to answering Van's questions. "It's as if she's hiding something," Aunt Jinny had said.

Harriet longed to find out what that something was. She might get her chance later that afternoon. Aunt Jinny had volunteered to take Ivy home from the hospital, and she'd suggested that Harriet meet them for lunch. Perhaps Harriet and her aunt could accomplish what Van could not.

During a break between appointments, Harriet left Polly in charge while she drove Skippy and Jiffy to the festival car park. The previous night, Skippy had been reluctant to leave Jiffy for even a minute, let alone the time it would take to drive there and back again. After Jiffy's episode, he didn't want Harriet to leave either, so she'd turned down Will's offer to retrieve the vehicle with her.

Since the parking spots on either side of Skippy's SUV were taken by other festivalgoers, Harriet maneuvered behind it in her grass-green Land Rover, a monstrosity which she affectionately referred to as "the Beast."

"Thanks for all ye did for my boy," Skippy said as he unbuckled his seat belt.

"Jiffy deserves all the credit for getting better."

When Jiffy had awakened before Harriet went to bed, Skippy took him on a short walk and fed him a handful of kibble. Harriet had checked on them and given Skippy strict instructions to call her if he needed anything before retiring to her room. But both man and dog had slept peacefully through the night. Thankfully, there'd been no more seizures, and Jiffy had enjoyed a light breakfast earlier that morning.

"He's a remarkable dog," she continued.

"That he is," Skippy said. "I suppose I got carried away telling stories about him last night."

"I enjoyed your stories." Harriet and Skippy had eaten leftover lasagna, salad, and breadsticks on TV trays while Jiffy rested in his kennel. The stories of Skippy and Jiffy's search and rescue exploits had Harriet's heart pounding as she anxiously awaited hearing the outcome. Skippy was a natural storyteller who'd probably told his stories dozens of times over the years. Yet not one sounded rehearsed or overdone.

"You're both heroes," she added, "and I'm glad we met. Though I'm sorry about the circumstances."

"Me too." Skippy shifted in the passenger seat to look back at Jiffy. "But he seems himself again, and for that I'm grateful to the Good Lord."

They chatted a moment more as they got out of the Beast. Skippy opened the rear door, and Jiffy jumped to the ground. His tail wagged as he leaned against Skippy's leg.

"The stitches will dissolve in a week or so. Don't forget to return for your follow-up appointment." Harriet handed Skippy the medicine bottle containing Jiffy's pain pills and reminded him of the instructions. "But if anything happens before then, call me. Any time, day or night."

"That I'll do."

She gave Jiffy a hug before he hopped into the back of the SUV as if he hadn't been rendered unconscious less than twenty-four hours ago. When she returned to her vehicle, she sat in the seat for a moment before putting the transmission into reverse. She blinked away unexpected tears of gratitude.

Jiffy wouldn't be leaving Skippy alone anytime soon.

Harriet arrived at Ivy's stone farmhouse—perhaps a mile or two from Cobble Hill Farm as the crow flies, but about four to five via the roads—with salads she'd picked up from a local pub, the Crow's Nest, and a vase of freshly cut mums from her own garden.

She parked the Beast behind Aunt Jinny's car and gazed at the two-story home. The flat front reminded her of the cottage where the Dashwood women went to live in *Sense and Sensibility*. To the characters in Jane Austen's classic novel, the cottage seemed small and cramped, especially compared to the mansion they were forced to leave. But Harriet had always thought it charming.

Both Ivy and Fern lived on the farm that had been in their family for generations. According to Aunt Jinny, Ivy had inherited the main house and the surrounding grounds, while the majority of the farmland and a stone cottage had been bequeathed to Fern. Most of the pasture was rented out to a neighboring farmer, all except a few acres where Fern raised her pet goats, chickens and guinea fowls, and prizewinning cabbages.

When Aunt Jinny told Harriet about the division of the property, she'd wondered if that had been the cause of the sisters' rivalry. Harriet knew she'd been blessed that no family resentment occurred when Grandad left her so much of his estate. Her father hadn't minded being passed over in the least. In fact, he'd encouraged Grandad to will his portion to Harriet. Her father had no intention of leaving his position as CFO of a successful corporation in Connecticut and was grateful he didn't have to make international trips to navigate the British probate system. Aunt Jinny and her son, Anthony, were relieved that Old Doc Bailey's veterinary legacy remained in the family and more than content with the inheritance bequeathed to them.

Carrying the takeaway bag and vase of flowers, Harriet followed a brick pathway from the driveway to the cement porch and knocked on the door. It appeared to have once been painted a vibrant green, but exposure to weather had caused the color to fade to an uneven muted shade.

The door opened, and Aunt Jinny welcomed her with a warm smile. "Come on in. Ivy is in the parlor, and we're both starving."

"Then I guess I'm right on time."

"You go say hello to Ivy." Aunt Jinny reached for the salads. "I'll sort these out and join you in a minute."

"Are you sure you don't need my help?"

"I can manage the food, and the table is already set. Go on now."

Harriet smiled as she entered the living area. Sunshine bathed the room in light through tall windows adorned with heavy upholstered drapes. Ivy rested in a wingback chair with her hands folded primly in her lap. Her rouged cheeks and bright lipstick didn't hide the dark shadows under her eyes or her sallow complexion.

"How are you feeling?" Harriet asked after her initial greeting. She braced herself for a brusque retort.

"Much better," Ivy replied, her tone cordial, even kind. "Especially now that I'm home instead of in the hospital. I know the nurses mean well, and they do their best, but the overnight stay was an unnecessary precaution. I would have slept much better in my own bed under my own roof."

"I'm not sure Aunt Jinny agreed with that."

"No, she didn't," Ivy said with a good-natured laugh.

Harriet held out the vase. "These are for you. Where should I put them?"

"How thoughtful." Ivy's eyes rounded in delight. "I've always loved mums. Please place them right here by me where I can soak in their beauty." She patted the oval table situated between her chair and a matching wingback. A crocheted doily covered most of the burnished surface, which held a lamp, a short stack of books, and other bits and bobs.

Harriet placed the vase beside the books and was delighted when Ivy gently touched one of the blossoms. She'd hoped Ivy would like the small gift.

"Autumn colors are so beautiful," Ivy said. "All the warm golds, oranges, and russets. I believe I appreciate them more the older I get. Perhaps it's because our life spans seem to follow the rhythms of a year and I'm entering the autumn of mine."

"I pray you have many years ahead of you, Ms. Chapman," Harriet said. She didn't want to think about where that analogy placed her. Late summer, perhaps? Was she living in her own September?

"After our adventure in the cave, I believe we're well enough acquainted for you to call me Ivy. May I call you Harriet? Or do you prefer Dr. Bailey?" A teasing spark shone in Ivy's weary eyes. "Though I suppose Young Doc Bailey might suit. I've heard you referred to that way a time or two."

"If that sticks, I suppose I'll get used to it," Harriet said with a smile. "But please call me Harriet."

"Have a seat then, Harriet." Ivy gestured to the chair on the other side of the table.

Harriet perched on the edge of the upholstered cushion, ready to jump up and give Aunt Jinny a hand when she joined them. "I'm glad your injuries weren't more serious."

"Apparently too serious for me to return to the festival this afternoon." Ivy eyed the kitchen door and raised her voice. "At least that's Dr. Bossy's professional opinion."

"I wouldn't have to be bossy if you would do what's best for your body, but here we are," Aunt Jinny called back.

Harriet smothered a giggle, and Ivy gave her a mischievous smile.

"I'll stay put for today, but I insist on going tomorrow." Ivy lowered her gaze, and her knuckles whitened. Her voice took on a frustrated edge. "Who knows what a mess Fern has made of the appraisals during my absence? There's an order and a process that must be strictly adhered to, but my sister doesn't know the meaning of those words."

Harriet was considering her response when Aunt Jinny came into the room carrying a tray with their salads. She'd transferred them from the takeaway boxes into glass bowls.

"I'm sure Fern is doing fine, and the appraisers already know what's expected of them," Aunt Jinny said as she placed the tray on the dining table, which was set with crystal water tumblers. "Now let's enjoy this lovely lunch, shall we?"

Ivy leaned toward Harriet and spoke in a stage whisper. "She's an optimist, that one. And as diplomatic as they come. We all know the truth about Fern's capabilities." Ivy struggled to rise, and Harriet rushed to escort her to the chair at the head of the table.

Once they were settled, Aunt Jinny said grace, thanking God for the food and asking His continued care during Ivy's recovery.

"Thank you," Ivy murmured as she laid her linen napkin in her lap. "For the prayer and for this beautiful luncheon."

"You're very welcome," Aunt Jinny said. "And please stop worrying about the appraisals. You'll have plenty of time in the morning to undo any mistakes Fern may have made."

"Mistakes Fern *did* make," Ivy insisted. "I only wish I knew how many 'mistakes' she makes on purpose to destroy the reputation of the appraisal program. She wants the festival to be all fun and games. No more antiques. No more finding the extraordinary amongst the ordinary."

"I'm sure that's not true," Aunt Jinny said. "Besides, the festival's reputation grows each year. Fern couldn't destroy it if she tried. You should tell Harriet about a few of those extraordinary finds."

For the rest of the meal, Ivy entertained her guests with stories of discovered treasures and frauds. Most people took the news that their family heirloom had little but sentimental value with grace and good humor. But a few adamantly disagreed with the appraiser.

"It seems the uglier the object, the angrier the owner gets," Ivy said, tears of laughter dampening her cheeks. She pretended to glare at Aunt Jinny. "I don't want any temper tantrums from you when you find out that gargoyle of yours is worthless."

"No tantrums." Aunt Jinny held up her hand. "I promise. Though I've grown quite fond of Winston since I found him. He's not going back into the attic."

"He's not going to a museum or auction house either," Ivy retorted.

"As if anyone could persuade me to part with him. Obviously, I'll have to award him a place of honor in my own home. You can come and visit him whenever you want," Aunt Jinny teased.

Harriet grinned at the women's good-natured banter. How she loved this aspect of village life.

When they'd finished, Harriet insisted on tidying up. As soon as the table was cleared and the kitchen cleaned, she joined the women in the parlor. Ivy once again sat in her wingback chair while Aunt Jinny relaxed in a corner of the upholstered couch.

"I should be going," Harriet said, not wanting to overstay her welcome or tire Ivy any further.

"Could you stay a little longer?" Aunt Jinny asked, eyeing their hostess. "Ivy has something to tell you."

That news didn't surprise Harriet. She'd expected there was more to the lunch invitation than friendly hospitality. But when they'd finished the meal without a hidden agenda being revealed, she'd begun to second-guess her instinct. Now it appeared her first inclination was correct.

She checked her watch. There was plenty of time before her next appointment. And Polly hadn't texted or called about any emergencies from the clinic.

"I can stay a bit longer." Trying to contain her curiosity, Harriet lowered herself into the chair next to Ivy, who flushed and averted her gaze. Was Ivy about to hand her another clue to the mystery attacker's identity?

"While we were driving home this morning, Ivy told me why she went to the cave," Aunt Jinny said quietly. "I asked her to tell you too."

Harriet shifted her gaze from her aunt to Ivy, whose cheeks were now bright red even without the help of her rouge. The uncomfortable silence lasted a long moment before Ivy sighed and picked up the top book in her stack. She pulled a folded sheet of paper from between its pages.

"I got this note," she said, staring pointedly at Aunt Jinny. "It's not a hallucination, and neither was that ghost knight."

"I believe you," Aunt Jinny said, as if she'd already said those words a hundred times before.

Ivy passed the note to Harriet. "You may read it to yourself. I don't wish to hear the words aloud."

Harriet unfolded a plain piece of white paper that had been torn in half. The typed words read:

Meet me at the cliffside cave, my dearest Ivy, for you are the greenery of my garden. See you at three when the tide is low and my spirits are high.

Harriet didn't dare meet her aunt's gaze. If she did, she'd wouldn't be able to hold back the laughter bubbling in her chest. Who had written such a ridiculous note? The obvious answer was whoever wanted to lure Ivy to the cave, but why would a woman of Ivy's good sense go there?

The answer came to Harriet with a pang of regret for her judgmental attitude. Ivy, like Harriet, longed for the love of a good man, the man God meant for her. Ivy had gone to the cave because of hope.

"Who did you think sent the note?" Harriet asked as she refolded the page.

Ivy averted her gaze. "A...dear friend. His name isn't important."

"Maybe it is," Harriet said. Especially if he'd lured Ivy to the cave to cause her harm. "Did he hand this to you? Ask someone else to deliver it?"

"I found it in my bag. I'd left it near the registration counter where anyone could have gotten into it." Ivy wrung her hands and shot a desperate look at Harriet, silently pleading for her to understand. "I guessed it was from him. But it couldn't have been, and I feel like a fool for even thinking that he'd want to meet me that way."

Harriet's heart ached for the older woman. Ivy had gone to the cave expecting to meet the man of her dreams in a romantic rendezvous, and instead she'd been the victim of someone's cruelty. She needed compassion not censure.

"Have you shown this to DC Worthington?" Harriet asked.

"I can't." Tears shimmered in Ivy's eyes. "He'd keep it as evidence, and then everyone would know of my foolishness."

"It wasn't foolishness," Aunt Jinny chimed in. "I admit that I'd be embarrassed too, but there's no need to be. Whoever sent that note is a bully and must be identified."

"There could be fingerprints on this note." Harriet frowned. "Including mine. I'm sorry, Ivy. If I'd thought about it, I'd have handled it more carefully."

"It's my note." Ivy took the folded paper from Harriet and returned it to her book. "No one is giving it to anyone else."

Harriet opened her mouth to argue, but Aunt Jinny stood. "Then there's nothing more to be said, and we mustn't delay Harriet any longer. I hate leaving you though. Are you sure you'll be all right on your own?"

"You're making too much of a fuss, Jinny, as you always do." Ivy waved a dismissive hand. "There's not a thing wrong with me that a little peace and quiet won't cure."

"I'll check in on you later then. I expect you to call if you need me."

"You have my word," Ivy assured her.

"Come along then, Harriet. You don't want to be late for your next appointment."

Though surprised at Aunt Jinny's sudden push to leave, Harriet accepted Ivy's gratitude for bringing lunch and thanked her for her hospitality. As she climbed into her vehicle, a thought nagged at the back of her mind, a connection she couldn't quite put together.

Did it have something to do with the mysterious typed note?

Harriet recited the words to herself as she wrestled with the Beast's transmission on her drive to the clinic. The writer apparently fancied himself a poet. She made a mental note to ask Aunt Jinny if she knew any men who might fit in Ivy's "dear friend" category who waxed poetic.

She also wanted to ask her aunt's advice on whether they should tell Van about the note. Not doing so gave her an uneasy feeling. What if he later charged them with withholding evidence? That would be awful.

A strange look had appeared in Ivy's eyes when she took the note from Harriet. Almost as if she knew something else that she was keeping to herself. Was she telling the truth about who she thought wrote the note? Did she plan to take matters into her own hands?

If so, she could be courting danger. How much more injury would she have suffered from the attacker if Jiffy hadn't shown up? Which led to another conundrum. Ivy had been missing for quite a while before Skippy and Jiffy arrived at the cave. Why was the mysterious ghost knight still there when Jiffy found her?

Or had Ivy waited all that time for a friend who never showed, and had then been an unfortunate victim of happenstance? Maybe she and Jiffy had simply been in the wrong place at the wrong time.

Neither scenario answered the primary questions. Who was the ghost knight, and what was he doing in the old pirate's cave?

CHAPTER SIX

During a break between appointments on Thursday morning, Harriet joined Polly at the receptionist's desk with two mugs of freshly brewed coffee, each with a splash of hazelnut creamer.

"Is this the way it is every September?" she asked as she lowered herself into a chair. She'd alternated between being extremely busy and comfortably busy in the months since she took over the practice. But the last couple of weeks hadn't been busy at all.

Polly tucked her dark hair—this week dyed with a streak of burnished orange—behind her ear and grinned. "Old Doc Bailey called it the lull between the storms. I think it's because families are settling back into their school routines. And then so many people, including the schools, are busy with the festival. They're either participating in the various activities or enjoying the carnival."

"That sounds like a plausible theory to me. I think it's great that the children can get out of school to perform."

"It's tradition," Polly explained. She sipped her coffee. She normally preferred tea, like any true Brit, but sometimes she indulged Harriet's "little American habit."

The twenty-four-year-old, with her prior experience as Grandad's receptionist, had been Harriet's lifesaver as she navigated reopening the veterinary clinic. Polly's organizational skills surpassed Harriet's own, and she could find even the most obscure, outdated file in mere seconds. Even more important, her engaging personality endeared her to everyone, even their most temperamental clients.

Polly knew all the stories of their beloved pets—whether they'd been bought, found, or rescued, the sicknesses they'd had, the mischief they'd gotten into, and a hundred other details. And not only for the dogs, cats, birds, and "pocket pets" either. She was also well acquainted with the local farming community and often gave Harriet guidance on which farmers needed only a word or two of advice as they vetted their own animals and those, usually hobby farmers, who required hands-on assistance for even routine care.

"Have you been enjoying the carnival?" Harriet asked.

"When I'm not here, I'm there." Polly's eyes sparkled. "Yesterday I was especially popular. Everyone wanted to know how Jiffy was doing after you single-handedly saved his life."

Harriet almost spit out her coffee. "I did no such thing. He had a small head wound, that was all."

"And multiple seizures."

"Two seizures. You must have read the report before you filed it."

Polly chuckled. "Details are quickly exaggerated in a village as vivacious as ours. From what I heard, the seizures lasted throughout the night and you never left his side."

"I hope you corrected them."

"I tried a couple of times, but then I gave up. It's not like it'll hurt your reputation for people to hear how dedicated you are. Besides, what people are saying about Ivy is even more unbelievable. The prevailing rumor is that a knight in shining armor struck her with his sword."

Harriet shook her head. "He wasn't wearing armor. Though he might have had on some kind of medieval costume." If only she could see that scrap of fabric again. Maybe if she told Van she needed it so she could update Jiffy's medical record, he'd arrange with the crime lab for her to get another peek. Though she'd described the scrap she'd found in the dog's mouth to the best of her ability, what if she'd gotten a detail wrong? After all, she had only held it for a few seconds before Skippy took it away from her.

Polly's eyes narrowed. "Are you saying there was a knight in the cave? I read about the fabric you found in Jiffy's mouth, but I assumed it was part of somebody's shirt."

"I suppose it could have been," Harriet said. "It was such a small piece, and yet it had an antiquated appearance. All I know is that Ivy said she saw a ghost knight."

"Why was she in the cave to begin with?"

"I can't say." Though Harriet trusted Polly to keep confidences, she couldn't break Ivy's trust. Besides, Polly didn't need to be added to Van's potential list of evidence-withholders. "But she had a reason."

Polly nodded, a gesture that assured Harriet that she didn't intend to press for an explanation. "I hope it was a good one, poor woman."

"It was." At least in Ivy's eyes. Who could fault her for accepting an invitation to a mysterious rendezvous in an ancient cave? Not Harriet, and she doubted a romantic like Polly would either.

Mysterious rendezvous.

The words echoed in Harriet's mind with the same persistence as the nagging feeling she'd had when she left Ivy's home the day before. Something she should remember.

It came to her later that day when the clinic closed and she waved goodbye to Polly, who pedaled toward the road on her bike.

Not a *mysterious rendezvous*, no. A *secret* one.

"Perhaps she had a secret rendezvous and forgot the time."

Those had been Fern's exact words, and she'd flushed when she'd said them. At the time, Harriet had thought Fern's embarrassment had come from a wish for a secret rendezvous of her own. But what if she'd flushed because she'd been the one who arranged the rendezvous?

But Fern wouldn't do that to her own sister.

Would she?

Harriet fought the horrible suspicion taking shape in her mind. The rivalry between the two women was no secret, and Fern had eagerly stepped into the emcee role when Ivy disappeared. Being in the spotlight had been more important to her than finding her sister.

What if Fern had written the note, knowing that Ivy couldn't resist the temptation to meet her "dear friend"? It didn't matter whether the relationship was real or imagined, at least not to Fern. Her sister longed for it to be true, so much so that she had temporarily abandoned her festival responsibilities to keep the supposed appointment.

In Harriet's imagining of the scenario, Fern bided her time then rushed to the volunteers on the veranda with the unlikely excuse that Ivy had wandered off. Unconcerned for her sister's welfare, Fern took over the stage. Later she'd seemed surprised that Ivy hadn't returned. And it wasn't until then that she'd suggested the secret rendezvous.

Had Fern offered that suggestion because she'd been the one to set it up?

Harriet didn't want to believe one sister could be so intent on stealing the spotlight from the other that she'd go to such measures, but history was full of sibling atrocities. *Look what Cain did to Abel and Jacob to Esau. What Joseph's brothers did to him.*

But Fern hadn't necessarily meant to cause her sister physical harm. Even if she had planted the note, that didn't mean she had anything to do with the ghost knight. Maybe she thought Ivy had decided to stay in the cave until her dear friend appeared, no matter how long that took and not knowing he'd never come. The longer Ivy stayed away, the more opportunity Fern had to shine on the stage.

"There's only one thing to do," Harriet said to Maxwell, who had accompanied her to the clinic entrance so he could get one final hug from Polly before she biked away. "I need to talk to Fern."

Perhaps she should call Aunt Jinny first. Her aunt would tell her if her suspicions were feasible, or if Harriet was thinking crazy thoughts.

From her vantage point standing outside the clinic, Harriet could see the parking area in front of the dower cottage where Aunt Jinny lived and maintained her medical practice. Her car wasn't there, which meant Aunt Jinny wasn't home. Perhaps she'd returned to Ivy's to check on her, or made any number of other house calls or errands.

Just as well. She might try to dissuade Harriet from talking to Fern. But how else could Harriet find out whether Fern had written the note? She couldn't tell Van her suspicions unless she was prepared to do so without Ivy's blessing. And she couldn't bring herself to do that.

Before she could talk herself out of her mission, Harriet changed clothes and drove to the festival grounds. With Ivy recuperating at home, albeit unhappily, Fern was sure to be lending a not-so-helpful hand to the committee organizers.

Not unsurprisingly, Harriet found Fern near the main stage where the local schoolchildren, adorable in their medieval costumes, recreated the historically significant Battle of Brunanburh. More than a millennia ago, in AD 937, England's King Æthelstan fought and defeated Constantine II, king of Scotland, and two of his allies in the famous battle.

The performance included moving speeches, heroic songs, and a shield wall. Harriet studied the costumes as best she could, but none of them were the same shade of red as the scrap of fabric. She hadn't really expected to find a child wearing the ghost knight's uniform, but one never knew when an unexpected clue would appear. She'd learned to be alert for such surprises over the past few months when one mystery after another had come her way.

When the performance ended, Fern took the stage to thank the children and announce that the White Church choir would be singing later that afternoon. "I hope to see you then," she said, her bright-red lips stretched in a huge smile as she lingered near the footlights. The smile faded as the benches in front of the stage emptied and proud parents reunited with their exuberant offspring. A moment later, Fern disappeared backstage.

Harriet found her in a covered area behind the stage where the various acts could wait until it was their turn to perform. Fern sat at an iron bistro table, staring at her phone.

"Mind if I join you?" Harriet took the other chair without waiting for an answer.

"Dr. Bailey," Fern said, her eyes wide. "I'm surprised to see you here. Shouldn't you be with Jiffy? Poor dog, suffering all those seizures. It must be a hardship for Skippy to endure such a sight."

Apparently, Polly hadn't been exaggerating about the overblown rumors.

"Jiffy had two seizures. He and Skippy went home yesterday morning, and he's doing quite well."

"I'm glad to hear it. Ivy is home too, which is such good news. I can't tell you how worried I've been about her. But all's well now, isn't it?"

Irritation burned in Harriet's chest. When Ivy first went missing, Fern hadn't seemed the least bit worried. Aunt Jinny had mentioned that Fern hadn't visited Ivy in the hospital. Neither had she shown up at the farmhouse, even though she lived on the property. How worried could Fern have been about her sister?

"I ate lunch with Ivy yesterday," Harriet said, managing to maintain a cordial tone. "She was so disappointed she can't be here today."

"I'm not surprised," Fern said. "She can't boss anyone around from her parlor, can she? But I'd say the festival is getting along fine without her. Better than it ever has before, in fact."

"That's good to hear. Since this is my first time, I don't know how it's been in the past or what to expect."

"No one expected Ivy to get herself bashed in the head by a ghost, I can tell you that." Fern emitted a harsh laugh. "What a story. But Ivy was always one to tell outlandish tales for attention."

"Why do you suppose she went to the cave?" Harriet leaned forward and crossed her arms on the metal table. She lowered her voice to a confidential whisper. "When we couldn't find Ivy, you said something about a secret rendezvous. Did she go there to meet someone?"

Fern's eyes lit up, and her lips curled into a huge smile. She obviously wanted Harriet to believe she had a secret—one she was dying to tell.

"It's possible she did," Fern said, drawing out the syllables. "Though I don't imagine she expected to meet a ghost."

"I feel sorry for her. Not only because of her injury, which was horrible enough, but because she's so embarrassed about the whole ordeal."

"As she should be," Fern declared. "What a fool she was, to fall for such a silly trick."

"What silly trick?"

Fern didn't reply, and Harriet bit her tongue to stop herself from saying something she shouldn't. She sensed that pressuring Fern for an answer was the wrong approach. Better to wait for her to talk first and see if she provided any clues.

As the silence between them intensified, Harriet purposely sat back, relaxed her shoulders, and rested her elbows on the arms of her chair. She breathed in the sea-scented breezes as if she hadn't a care in the world. Meanwhile, Fern fidgeted in her seat and shot sidelong glances her way.

"She got an anonymous note," Fern finally said, staring at Harriet as if to gauge her reaction to this news.

"What?" Harriet's tone mixed surprise and curiosity. At least she hoped it did. "How strange."

Fern looked around as if to ensure they were alone then bent toward Harriet. "I saw it," she stage-whispered.

"What did it say?" Harriet whispered in return, realizing that Fern had made a mistake in confessing this.

"It was quite poetic. The words were definitely intended to touch someone's heart."

Harriet pressed her lips together. If the note she'd read was Fern's idea of romance, that insight alone bolstered her suspicion that Fern was its author.

"Have you mentioned this to Van?"

"The detective constable?" Fern emitted a most unladylike snort. "Why should I? It's Ivy's business, not mine."

"True," Harriet agreed. "But it's all so odd, don't you agree?"

"If you knew Ivy as well as I did, you wouldn't think it odd at all. She falls for any man who shows her the slightest attention."

"I didn't mean Ivy." Harriet allowed a small smile. "Her actions are understandable. I was talking about you."

"Me?" Fern's cheeks flushed, but her gaze remained steady. "I'm sure I don't know what you're trying to insinuate. I've done nothing wrong."

Time for a direct attack. Harriet kept her tone soft and friendly while bracing herself for Fern's reaction. "You said you saw the note. But you haven't visited Ivy since her accident, which means you saw it before she went and you knew she had gone to the cave. But you didn't tell anyone, even when we were all running around trying to find her."

"That's not true—"

"Of course it is. I was there when you said Ivy had disappeared. But you didn't tell us about a note or that she'd gone to the cave."

Fern glared at Harriet, her mouth set in an angry line and her features turned to stone.

In for a penny, in for a pound.

Harriet took a deep breath and continued. "Even when Skippy arrived and organized the search party, you said nothing about a secret rendezvous. Is that because you wrote the note?"

Fern's jaw dropped, and she shoved to her feet, knocking her chair to the ground in her haste. "I refuse to listen to any more of your nonsensical accusations."

"I understand you're upset." Harriet stood also. "And I'm sorry about that. But I think DC Worthington needs to know about this conversation."

"You wouldn't dare tell him."

Harriet didn't respond. Nor did she shy away from Fern's scornful glare.

Fern righted her chair then dropped into it and buried her face in her hands. "I didn't mean for Ivy to get hurt," she said, her voice muffled. "I wanted her to go away for a while so I could have a turn as emcee. No one else was supposed to be in that cave. I don't know who attacked her."

Harriet touched Fern's shoulder. "I believe you. But someone *was* in that cave, someone who knew Ivy would be there. Tell me who else knew about the note."

Fern glanced toward Harriet, her eyes brimming with tears. "I'm not stupid. No one else knew. It was a complete coincidence that someone else was there. Maybe Ivy came close to finding a modern-day hideout or some kind of ghost cult." Fern gripped Harriet's arm, her fingers digging into the skin, and her voice rose in panic. "She's probably lucky to be alive. What if they come after her again?"

"I don't think that will happen," Harriet said, trying to reassure her. "Hopefully you're right that it was a coincidence. I'd hate to think that someone followed Ivy to the cave on purpose."

Fern appeared to be deep in thought as her demeanor changed from repentant and concerned sister to eager detective. "Ivy has made many enemies over the years," she said. "Perhaps she broke the camel's back by adding one last straw."

Though Harriet doubted Ivy had costumed enemies in the village, she didn't want to alienate Fern. The mercurial woman seemed to be on her side for the moment, and Harriet needed to keep her there.

"Is there anyone in particular who was angry with her?" she asked.

Fern tapped her fingers together and struck a thoughtful pose. "I do know," she said, her voice low and mysterious, "that Ivy argued with someone an hour or so before she left for the cave. None other than Wes Brinley."

"I don't know him."

Fern snorted at Harriet's ignorance. "He owns Uniquities, the antique and decor store on Seadog Street."

Harriet recognized the name of the store. "I've been in there." She'd been window-shopping after running a couple of errands, and her attention had been caught by a pair of candlesticks in the window. She'd gone inside and discovered a variety of antiques and elegant objets d'art. The items were charmingly arranged on polished shelves and tables, behind the glass doors of curio cabinets, and on the walls. Instead of the candlesticks, Harriet had purchased a glazed bowl that caught her fancy and now held fresh fruit on her kitchen counter.

"A woman with strawberry blond hair waited on me," she said.

"That's Emma, Wes's cousin. She's the business brains behind their success while Wes is handy at acquiring their inventory."

"Do you know what he and Ivy were arguing about?"

"I was otherwise engaged during that time," Fern said in a prim tone. "Someone else told me about the argument after Ivy was taken to the hospital. She didn't know why they were arguing though."

"Anyone I know?" Harriet said lightly, hoping Fern would relish another chance to share her superior knowledge.

"That depends on whether you know Heidi Paxton. I'm guessing you don't."

Harriet shook her head. "Who is she?"

"One of our expert appraisers." Fern composed her features into a broad smile that lacked any warmth. "In fact, she may be appraising whatever you entered into the show. I'd be careful about trying to charm her the way you've attempted to charm me. Heidi can always spot a fake."

Could an umbrella stand truly be a fake? Whether it was an antique or not hardly mattered, as long as it did its job.

Harriet shifted away from that rabbit trail and back to Fern. "All I want to do is find out who attacked Ivy and Jiffy."

"Leave that to the DC." Fern stood, her posture rigid. "One more thing," she added as she glared at Harriet. "If you tell Ivy or anyone else that I wrote that note, you'll have me for an enemy. Believe me, you don't want that."

Stunned by the threat, Harriet remained rooted where she stood while Fern flounced off as if she didn't have a care in the world. Which made Harriet wonder. Had Fern told the truth about the argument Heidi had supposedly witnessed between Ivy and Wes?

Or was she trying to distract Harriet's attention away from a crucial piece of evidence?

Fern had written the note to Ivy, but what had been her true motive? To get her sister away from the festival so she could shine in the spotlight? Or something more sinister?

CHAPTER SEVEN

Since she had no more appointments or any farm calls to make, Harriet wandered around the festival grounds, indulging in a funnel cake and pink cotton candy, while trying to come up with the best plan for getting information from two strangers—Wes Brinley and Heidi Paxton.

She halted by the carousel, her spirits lifted by the sight of children astride the gaily painted horses and circus animals. Most were laughing or smiling, though a few of the younger ones appeared nervous. One little boy kept his hand on the forearm of the man standing next to him as if the contact gave him courage.

Sometimes that was all it took, the touch of a friend. An encouraging word. A whisper from God. With such a gift, a person might garner the strength to pack up all of her belongings and move thousands of miles from her hometown. With such a gift, a person might have the courage to stay in her new home despite an intense longing to return.

When the carousel made another circuit, she noticed the boy and the man waving to one of the onlookers, a twentysomething woman with another child on the way. The young mother waved enthusiastically as she took photos of the duo with her phone.

In that moment, Harriet's heart ached for what she didn't have—a husband to take their child on a carousel. An experience she might never have, since her marital prospects had shattered.

Is this why I'm homesick? Because I'm still mourning the breakup?

She let the questions settle within her while she waited for the toddler and his dad to pass by her again. This time, a huge smile brightened the boy's face, though his hand remained on his dad's arm.

A simple touch.

Fear turned to courage.

The breakup still saddened her, but the end of that chapter in her life was not the end of her story.

She still struggled with a question she'd often pondered but never answered to her own satisfaction. What if she'd still been engaged when she learned of her grandfather's bequest? If she hadn't taken over his practice, the portion of the farm that hadn't been left to Aunt Jinny might have been sold. After all, Harriet's fiancé was a respected veterinarian in Connecticut. She couldn't imagine he'd ever consider starting over with her in Yorkshire.

And yet, how could she have sold her estate? Allowed a stranger to live in Grandad's house and possibly treat Grandad's clients? Who would have taken in Maxwell and Charlie?

Okay, that last one was easy. Either Polly or Aunt Jinny would have made sure the clinic dog and the office cat had good homes. But Harriet would never have known their love and affection.

The bottom line, it seemed, was that the inheritance might have led to *her* breaking the engagement. She could give sincere thanks to God that she hadn't been forced to make that decision. In His providence, He'd provided a silver lining in her cloud of gloom.

So no. She didn't want to go back to Connecticut in hopes of mending a broken relationship. But she did miss her parents and her friends and the familiarity of her growing-up years. She missed *home*.

And that was okay. Wasn't it?

"Tuppence for your thoughts?"

Startled by the male voice at her shoulder, Harriet spun. She smiled to see Pastor Will.

"I'm not sure they're worth that much." One side of her mouth quirked up. "Well, that's not true. They're worth much more than that. But only to me."

"I can tell," Will said, his hazel eyes exuding warmth. "I called your name twice, but I don't think you heard me. At least, I hope you weren't purposely ignoring me."

"Not at all." She noticed he was without his clerical collar and casually dressed in khakis and a knitted sweater. "Are you here to ride the rides?"

"I thought I'd stop here for my supper. Perhaps take a ride on the Ferris wheel if I can find someone to accompany me. Interested?"

"The Ferris wheel, huh?" Harriet bit her lip as she stared up at the giant wheel. She had a fear of those swaying seats, especially when they halted at the very top. At least the carnival's ride wasn't nearly as tall as the famous Ferris wheel in London. No one could talk her into riding that one.

"I hear the view of the sea is breathtaking," Will cajoled.

Harriet's mind flashed to the toddler who'd been fearful of the carousel and how a simple touch had given him courage. Surely she could be as brave as he'd been, especially with Will sitting next to her. Maybe even sitting close enough for their shoulders to touch.

"I'll be brave," she said.

Will laughed. "I didn't know it was a question of courage. I'll say a special prayer for our safe return to the ground."

"Then I'd be honored to accept your invitation." Harriet eyed the giant wheel one more time. "Ride first, then supper?"

"Excellent suggestion."

The lines for the rides were short at this time of day, a relatively quiet hour between the afternoon activities and the crush of the evening crowds. Before Harriet had garnered sufficient courage, the ride operator motioned for her to take a seat. Though perhaps that was for the best, since it didn't give her the chance to change her mind.

A few seconds after the ride started, it stopped, and their seat swung back and forth. Harriet squealed and grabbed Will's arm.

He grinned and placed his hand on hers. "'Be strong and of good courage,'" he said, quoting the Old Testament book of Joshua.

She shut her eyes. "I'm trying."

Will nudged her as they rose upward again. "Look at the sea."

Harriet forced her eyes open. She straightened, causing the seat to sway again, but this time she barely noticed the movement. The sun, low in the western sky, cast long shadows into the depths of the deep-sea waters. "Oh, Will. It's breathtaking."

He gave her an amused smile. "God's paintbrush sweeps across the skies."

"Yes." A deep sigh escaped Harriet, and she relaxed in the seat. The magnificent view was worth the unsettled feeling in her stomach. Amazingly, the longer they rode, the more she enjoyed it, especially as day softened to dusk. She didn't even mind when their seat stopped at the top.

She peered over the side to the ground below, exulting in how daring she felt, and was dazzled by the bright colorful lights. The festivalgoers meandered like an animated collection of miniature dolls. As the ride inched forward then stopped again as people got off and on, she returned her attention to the sky to seek out the moon. It peeked between the wisps of a slow-moving cloud, slender and pale.

"You're enjoying this," Will said.

"Immensely."

"Enough to go again?"

"Do you want to?"

"Why not?"

They rode the Ferris wheel one more time then ventured to a couple of the other rides. Afterward, they made their way to the food booths. They purchased sausage rolls and sodas from a local vendor then found seats across from each other at one of the picnic tables scattered around the area.

"I'm glad I ran into you here," Will said as he squeezed a packet of spicy mustard onto his sausage roll. "This is fun."

"For me too." While they'd been riding the Ferris wheel, Harriet had pushed aside her conversation with Fern. The reprieve had been welcome. But now she was reminded that there was a mystery to solve and she had her next lead, questioning two strangers.

Strangers to her, but maybe not strangers to Will. Or to Aunt Jinny or Polly. Any one of the three could help obtain the answers Harriet needed. Though maybe she should find a way to talk to Wes and Heidi on her own without involving anyone else.

Then again, why would either of them talk to her? She couldn't mention Ivy's note without breaking a confidence, and Fern's assertion of an argument between her sister and Wes was based on hearsay. Heidi could be mistaken about what she witnessed. For all Harriet knew, Fern had made the whole thing up. Either way, the argument might not have taken place at all, and she couldn't ask Wes about it based on gossip. She let out a sigh.

"There you go again," Will said. "Lost in thought while I prattle on about the history of the Ferris wheel."

"I'm sorry. It's just—" She pressed her lips together, unable to give him an explanation. "You have my full attention now. What were you saying?"

"I was showing off my vast knowledge of useless trivia." His eyes gleamed with warm understanding. "I heard you had lunch with Ivy yesterday. She enjoyed your visit."

"Have you seen her?"

"I stopped there for a cuppa on my way here." His expression turned thoughtful. "You can't stop thinking about the mysterious ghost knight, can you?"

"Guilty." She gave him an apologetic smile. "Though I am sorry I didn't hear what you said about the Ferris wheel. I enjoyed it much more than I expected to."

"The history lesson can wait. What do you know about Ivy's mystery attacker that you aren't saying?"

Harriet hesitated a moment, pondering how to answer his question without breaking Ivy's confidence. Finally, she shrugged. "Gossip, honestly."

"Gossip from Fern?"

Harriet was dumbfounded. "How did you know?"

He tapped his temple with a finger. "I'm observant and intuitive."

She tilted her head and narrowed her eyes while allowing a small smile. "Did Fern say something to you?" Harriet immediately held up both hands, waving them in the air as if erasing her words. "Don't answer that. I shouldn't have asked, and you wouldn't have brought up her name if she had."

"I'm glad you know that about me," Will said, his tone more serious now than it had been before. "Though you've confirmed something I suspected."

"What's that?"

"Fern was at Ivy's house when I arrived, and she couldn't get out of there fast enough. She was embarrassed to see me and barely spoke a word. Not typical Fern behavior."

"I imagine not." Harriet couldn't help wondering if Fern had told Ivy that she'd written the note. And how had Ivy responded to her sister's trickery? "Did Ivy tell you anything about Fern's visit? I mean anything that isn't confidential."

"She complained about Fern's handling of the antique registrations."

"So, nothing new."

"Are you able to tell me what Fern told you? Without breaking a confidence, of course," he added with a teasing grin.

Harriet took a sip of her soda to avoid giving an immediate answer. Though what harm could it do to tell Will what Fern had said? Not about the note—she'd keep Fern's misdeed to herself—but about the argument.

"Someone told Fern that Ivy argued with a man named Wes Brinley about an hour before she disappeared. Do you know him?"

"We chat now and then. Neither he nor his cousin, Emma, attend White Church. I bought my mum's Christmas present at their store last year. A pair of hand-carved bookends dating to the early 1800s."

"What an unusual gift. Your mother must love books."

"You should see her library." He opened the small bag of chips that came with their meals, which he would have called crisps. "What was the argument about?"

"Fern didn't say. And since she didn't witness it herself, I can't even be sure it happened."

"Who did Fern say witnessed it?"

"An appraiser, Heidi Paxton."

"I think I've met her, though I can't say for sure. The appraisers come from all around the UK, and most come back year after year," he said. "Does Van know about this argument?"

"I doubt it. Fern told me because she realized I suspected that she knew why Ivy had gone to the cave." Had that sentence even made sense? Nothing like dancing around the details.

Will's gaze was long and lingering as he ate. He knew she was being evasive—that was obvious—but, thankfully, he didn't pry. As someone who was often privy to others' secrets, he respected confidentiality.

"That's something I've wondered too," he said at last. "I asked Ivy why she went there, but she got all huffy and changed the subject. I'm glad she confided in you."

"I asked her to tell Van. But she doesn't seem inclined to do so." Harriet frowned. "Maybe we should talk about something else before I say too much."

"I agree. No more talk about why Ivy went to the cave. But that doesn't mean we can't talk about the argument."

"I've already told you everything I know about that. Which isn't anything at all."

"But you want to know more about it, and so do I," he said enthusiastically. "We could go see Ivy and ask her about it."

"She'd want to know how I know. I'd rather not tell her about my conversation with Fern. Not yet." Though Harriet supposed Ivy would eventually learn that Fern had written the note—if she didn't know already—she didn't want to be the one to tell her.

Will peered past her. "Then we talk to the other person involved. Wes Brinley. Who happens to be standing right there." He nodded toward something behind her.

Harriet twisted around on the bench and spotted a man in line at a food truck. While waiting, he alternated between tapping at his phone and scanning the crowd. He seemed oblivious to Harriet and Will.

Wes wasn't exceptionally tall, but he had a lanky build. Thick brown hair stood upright in gelled tufts that framed a thin face and narrow jaw. Dark eyes peered through wire-rimmed glasses in rounded frames. Harriet couldn't decide whether he was going for an edgy or sophisticated style. Maybe something in between.

"Why would he tell us anything?" she asked Will. "He doesn't even know me."

"I imagine he's heard of you," Will said. "Your arrival in White Church Bay caused quite a stir and was the conversation of many a teatime encounter. Trust me, I was witness to several."

Harriet knew that was true. Grandad, a beloved member of the local community, had been mourned by his friends, neighbors, and clients. The news that he'd bequeathed his house and his practice to his American granddaughter had the Yorkshire tongues wagging but also resulted in Harriet being warmly welcomed to her new home. At least by most people. A few farmers were wary of her "Yankee ways," but she was slowly earning their trust.

"I can't just come out and ask him if he argued with Ivy," she protested.

"Leave that to me. Wait here."

Will left his seat and sauntered over to Wes, who was exchanging coins for a red-and-white striped box of popcorn and a bottle of soda. Harriet couldn't hear what they were saying, but she smiled when Wes glanced in her direction. A moment later, the two men joined her at the table.

"Emma, my cousin and business partner, said you've stopped in at Uniquities," Wes said after Will introduced them. "I'm sorry I wasn't there to meet you."

"It's a lovely shop. So many unusual items."

"That's our specialty. If you can't find what you're looking for someplace else, then you're looking in the wrong place." He opened the box of popcorn as he sat across from Harriet and Will. "Which is why we encourage everyone to come to us first. We're sure to have the perfect item for that special gift, either for yourself or someone else."

Harriet couldn't help being in awe of Wes's canned patter. Did he always respond to an introduction with a commercial message? She faked a smile and avoided making eye contact with Will. If she did, she might not be able to keep her laughter inside where it belonged.

"I'll remember that," she managed to say.

"Emma and I don't have any pets," Wes went on. "Not even a picturesque cat to curl up on a shelf of antiques. Emma's allergic to pet dander, and I—" He tilted his head and frowned. "Guess I've always been too busy to take care of an animal."

Though she'd had similar conversations multiple times during her veterinary career, Harriet never quite understood why people felt a need to explain to her why they didn't have a pet. Almost as if they were compelled to apologize.

She resorted to her pat answer. "Pets aren't for everybody." Short, sweet, and to the point.

"I suppose not."

"Did you hear about the search and rescue dog that was injured a couple of days ago?" Will asked, his voice as casual as if he were chatting about the weather. "He was called in to search for Ivy Chapman, and both of them were attacked."

Wes frowned. "Hard to miss that helicopter flying overhead on its way to the hospital. How is Ivy?"

"Home now," Will replied. "She plans to be here tomorrow to be sure the appraisal process goes smoothly."

"I'm glad to hear it. The festival isn't the same without her." Wes shifted his gaze to Harriet. "What about the dog? Someone said it had a lot of seizures."

"Just two," Harriet answered. "He's doing fine now."

"That's good."

"Did you enter anything to be appraised?" Will asked Wes. "I imagine you'd have a large variety of antiques to choose from."

"True," Wes said, his thin lips spreading into a superior smile. "But after all of our years in business, Emma and I know what our stock is worth. You need to have an eye for that kind of thing if you want to keep your doors open. Emma and I have that eye."

"I suppose you do," Will said. He chuckled. "I know nothing about business or antiques. I merely thought that having something in the show might be good publicity for your shop."

Wes shoved a handful of popcorn into his mouth, his shoulders tensing as he chewed. When he finished, he closed the box. "We get plenty of customers during the Antique Festival. People come to see what's being appraised then visit the village to shop."

"I haven't been to the pavilion yet," Will said. He turned to Harriet. "Have you?"

"Not since day before yesterday when Aunt Jinny and I dropped off our items," Harriet said. "Ivy gushed over my umbrella stand." She grinned. "But she was not impressed by Aunt Jinny's gargoyle."

"I hope she didn't offend Dr. Garrett," Wes said. "Ivy can be a crusty old bird when she gets her feathers ruffled."

"So I've heard," Will put in. "In fact, I understand you had a run-in with her that day."

Wes snorted, a wary expression in his eyes. "Did she tell you that?"

Will didn't answer but held his gaze steady. Harriet took another sip of her soda, feeling uncomfortable. Wes wasn't likely to give them answers if he felt threatened.

"I should have known she'd make a big deal out of nothing," he said at last. "Sure, I lost my temper. But I didn't attack her. Did she tell the DC it was me?"

"Not that I'm aware of," Will said, his tone friendly and sympathetic. "What did she get so mad about?"

"It was ridiculous. Such a lot of fuss and bother." He rolled his eyes as if frustrated that he had to explain himself. "I was less than honest a moment ago, Pastor. I have been to the pavilion. Truth is, Ivy stopped in the shop a couple of weeks ago and became enamored with a bronze sculpture we had on display called *Three Dogs at Night*. Not enamored enough to buy it, you understand. But she wanted to showcase it in the appraisal exhibit. I agreed, because why not? Like you said, publicity and all."

"Sure," Will said.

Wes tapped his soda bottle on the picnic table a few times as if the gesture calmed him. "Anyway, Emma gave it to her a day or two before registration opened. But when I stopped by the pavilion to see how it was displayed, Ivy said Emma hadn't brought it in. When I insisted she had, Ivy accused me of lying. Then I accused her of either losing the sculpture or deciding to keep it for herself."

"I see," Will said.

Wes held up a hand. "I know it was wrong of me, and I was sorry afterward. Then, when I found out about the attack…" He let the words trail off.

"It's not like Ivy to make accusations like that," Will said, seeming to direct his words more to Harriet than to Wes. "I mean, she has little patience with Fern, but why should she accuse Emma of lying when it must have been a misunderstanding?"

"I guess the sculpture was important to her," Harriet said. "Why is it called *Three Dogs at Night*?"

"I'll show you a photo." Wes pulled out his phone and tapped the screen. "It's a bronze sculpture of a trio of Labrador retrievers next to a tree with the moon caught in its branches."

When he found what he was looking for, he passed the phone to Harriet. The screen displayed the Uniquities website gallery. Wes had enlarged the photo of the sculpture. She held the phone so both she and Will could examine the image.

"It's a striking piece," Harriet said. "Is it valuable?"

"I'm not sure," Wes said with a shrug.

Harriet hid her surprise. Moments before, Wes had bragged about his ability to evaluate the worth of the items he sold in his shop. Now he casually admitted the opposite. But that wasn't important right now. Harriet was more interested in knowing why Ivy had been so upset.

She slid Wes's phone across the table to him. "Do you know why this particular sculpture mattered so much to Ivy?"

"She wanted to show it to a collector who might be interested in it." He pocketed the phone. "She didn't give me a name."

Of course she didn't. Poor Ivy.

Harriet's heart ached for the older woman. She might be adding one and one and getting three, but she didn't think so. Her intuition told her why Ivy was upset. Not that she could explain her reasoning to either Will or Wes.

To Harriet, it was obvious that Ivy wanted to show *Three Dogs at Night* to a specific collector who was also the "dear friend" she thought had written the note.

Ivy probably envisioned herself and the collector enjoying a quiet moment in the pavilion together studying the sculpture. A moment that wouldn't have the same ambiance if it took place among the shelves and displays at Uniquities with Wes or Emma hovering in the background.

"There's nothing more I can tell you," Wes said. "Only that Emma says she gave the sculpture to Ivy and Ivy says she didn't."

"You mean you still haven't found it?" Harriet asked, unable to keep the surprise from her voice.

"Nope." Wes slid from the bench. "I need to get going. It was nice meeting you, Dr. Bailey. I hope you'll stop in at Uniquities again soon."

"I'll do that. Thank you."

Will stopped him. "One last thing, Wes."

"What is it, Pastor?"

"I was wondering if you were involved in the search for Ivy? I mean before Skippy and Jiffy arrived?"

"No." Wes's eyes narrowed. "Why do you ask?"

"If Ivy told DC Worthington about the argument, he'll want to know where you were when she disappeared."

"If he asks, I'll tell him." Without another word, Wes tossed the popcorn box into a nearby dustbin and disappeared into the crowd.

"What do you think?" Will asked Harriet. "Could Wes be the ghost knight?"

"I couldn't say." Another question preoccupied her thoughts.

If Wes and Emma no longer had the sculpture and neither did Ivy, then who did?

Harriet's imagination took a giant leap. What if Ivy's dear friend, the collector, had stolen *Three Dogs at Night*? What if the missing sculpture was the key to everything else that had happened?

CHAPTER EIGHT

After the clinic closed on Friday afternoon, Harriet and Polly drove to one of the designated lots at the top of the hill that sloped to the North Sea. Harriet parked the Beast and gazed through the windshield at the rooftops of the quaint village.

White Church Bay was situated between two steep cliffs. It dated to the early 1500s, though its origins reached even further back into history. Norwegians and Danes, the much-feared Vikings, settled in the area about a thousand years after Jesus's birth. Though the church and newer houses had been built at the top of the cliff, the shops and older homes lined a maze of streets that were too narrow to accommodate modern vehicles. Only tradespeople and emergency vehicles could navigate them.

"Are you ready for the downward trek?" Polly asked with a teasing lilt.

"I'm looking forward to it." Harriet grabbed her bag and slid from the driver's seat. When she first arrived at her new home, she'd found the cobblestone path that led to the lower section of the village daunting. But within a few weeks, she'd developed calf muscles unlike any she'd ever had before and she could walk back and forth to the parking lot without getting out of breath.

At least not too much.

"I can't thank you enough for coming with me." Polly adjusted the strap of her cross-body bag. "Especially when you have so many other things on your mind."

"Mostly I want to know who attacked Ivy and Jiffy." That was the primary mystery. It would be easier if she knew which clues truly mattered, as well as what other clues she needed to find. "Besides," Harriet continued, "I have a couple of errands to run after our mani-pedis."

Including a stroll past Uniquities. The shop would probably be closed by the time she casually wandered by and paused to peer through the window. She had no idea what she hoped to accomplish except for a minuscule chance she'd see the alleged missing sculpture on display.

Though Harriet didn't want to accuse Emma or Wes of lying, she believed Ivy over them. They'd be foolish to keep the sculpture in the shop after accusing Ivy of taking it. But people sometimes did foolish things. Besides, even if the sculpture wasn't there, clues often appeared where they were least expected.

At the salon, Harriet and Polly sipped fruity mocktails while relaxing in comfy massage chairs. Their legs, hands, and arms were pampered with lavender scrubs, moisturizers, and hot stones. Polly chose a rich burgundy polish for her toes and a black-and-white ombre look for her fingernails. Harriet's choices weren't as bold. By the time they left, her fingernails sported a pale mauve shellac while her toenails, hidden from view by thick socks and ankle boots, were a few shades darker.

"I'm stopping by the bakery to pick up a few items for Mum," Polly said as she pulled a stocking cap over her orange-streaked hair. "She made broccoli cheddar soup for supper and wants to serve it in bread bowls. You're welcome to join us if you'd like."

"Don't you have a date to go to the festival with—oh, what's his name? The young man with the ferrets."

"He canceled." Polly's flippant tone held no regret.

"Wasn't he the reason for these?" Harriet wiggled her fingers to indicate their new manicures.

"These," Polly said, giggling as she imitated the gesture, "are for me. And since I've been to the festival every night this week—"

"And with a different man each time." Harriet's usually dormant matchmaking antennae sparked to life. "Perhaps Van could go with you. He could probably use a bit of fun."

"I've already made other plans." Polly's gray eyes sparkled with amusement. She never minded being teased about her dating life. The men who took her out were strictly friends, she'd told Harriet once. Friends to have a good time with while waiting for the right one to come along. Harriet secretly thought Van might be the "right one," but Polly didn't seem to think so. At least not yet.

"With Dad gone off to London for a business trip," Polly continued, "Mum and I are curling up with our bread bowls and a movie. You're more than welcome to join us. Mum always makes enough soup for a small army."

"That's a tempting offer, but maybe another time. I need to stop by the library before it closes to pick up a book they're holding for me, and then I'd like to do a little window-shopping."

"See you tomorrow then." Polly hummed a popular tune as she sauntered toward the bakery while Harriet went in the opposite direction.

It took a few moments to check out the book, a mystery by one of her favorite authors. Apparently, it was a favorite among many of the library's patrons, since there'd been a wait for the limited number of copies. Harriet had been delighted to finally get the email saying her turn had come. Maybe she'd spend her Friday evening with Maxwell and a pizza. She could lose herself in the pages of the mystery while the dachshund snoozed beside her.

She tucked the novel in her bag and left the library. Instead of heading for the pizza place, though, she took a meandering detour past Uniquities. With fall came the end of the tourist season, which meant most of the village's shops no longer stayed open in the evenings. The locals shopped during the day, so late hours weren't worth the merchants' while.

Like many other businesses on this cobblestone street, Uniquities was located in a one-story sandstone cottage that had been renovated decades ago. The Biscuit Bistro and Calabash Insurance Agency were nearby, along with a few other specialty shops. None of them were open, and only a handful of people were out and about on the quiet street.

She paused beside the large bay window where she'd noticed the candlesticks months before and admired the autumn-themed display. A variety of lanterns, vases, urns, and even an antique cider press shared the space with tastefully arranged pumpkins, gourds, and fall flowers. Strands of tiny yellow and white lights added a warm ambiance.

Beyond the display, a variety of furniture—desks, dressers, upholstered chairs—was visible in the dim glow of the shop's security lights. Was *Three Dogs at Night* also inside? Harriet couldn't know unless she jimmied the lock and searched the premises.

A crime she wasn't willing to commit.

As she turned to head back up the sloping path to the car park, her attention was caught by the Biscuit Bistro sign that jutted above the entrance. Poppy's coral rose cookie jar had gone missing with no sign of a break-in. Perhaps the cookie jar thief had also stolen the bronze sculpture.

But then why wouldn't Wes have said so, instead of accusing Ivy of losing or stealing it herself? Unless he didn't know the cookie jar had gone missing.

Questions without answers. But none of them as vital to uncover as the identity of the ghost knight. After all, he had already proven dangerous.

A siren sounded in the distance, growing louder as it neared. Another siren joined the cacophony of the first. Harriet seemed rooted to the sidewalk as she waited to see if the emergency vehicles turned on this street. A moment later, as if she'd summoned it, one did.

The detective constable's official vehicle screeched to a stop in front of Uniquities, and Van slid from the driver's seat. An ambulance followed close behind.

"Harriet?" Van asked, apparently astonished to find her outside the store. "Did you make the 999 call? Were you inside?" His questioning tone matched the puzzled expression on his face, as if something didn't make sense.

"The store's closed," Harriet answered as she recalled that 999 was the emergency number in the UK. "I didn't call anyone. What's happened?"

Two medics from the ambulance joined them, and Van tried the door handle, but it wouldn't open. "Locked from the inside," he murmured. He shaded his eyes and peered through the glass. "I see him. Stand back, everybody."

One of the medics herded Harriet behind the DC's cruiser, but she turned in time to see Van shielding his eyes as he smacked the door window with his nightstick. She tensed and ducked her head at the sound of shattering glass.

"Who's in there?" she asked the medic. Van had said *him*. "Is it Wes?"

Instead of answering, the medic joined his colleague. Together, they followed Van into the shop. Harriet hesitated but soon made up her mind to see the scene for herself. After all, Wes was a possible suspect in the attack on Ivy and Jiffy. Not that Van knew that. Yet.

The shattered glass glistened on the sidewalk and in the store's entryway. The medics and Van bent over someone lying on the floor in front of a bookcase that displayed vintage hats and gloves. Though she couldn't see the unconscious victim's face, Harriet guessed him to be Wes based on what she could see of his lanky body. Whether he'd merely passed out or something nefarious had occurred, she couldn't tell.

Beside the cash register was a landline phone. The receiver lay beside it, and a faint voice could be heard coming through the open line. Van picked up the receiver, said a few words too quietly for Harriet to hear, and then hung up. He looked up and saw her standing behind the medics. "This is a crime scene. You shouldn't be in here."

"Isn't there anything I can do to help?"

He pointed to the door where a few bystanders were craning their necks to see what was happening inside the store. "I could use a hand setting up a perimeter while the medics tend Mr. Brinley."

"What happened to him?"

"I don't know. When dispatch answered the emergency call, he didn't say anything." Van's eyes narrowed as he looked from Wes to the counter. Harriet followed his gaze, mentally measuring the distance between the two. If Wes had made the call, then fallen, he'd be closer to the counter. Even if he'd taken a step or two first and then stumbled, wouldn't he still have the receiver in his hand? Or maybe it would have been dangling by its cord. Instead, it had been next to the phone.

Harriet stared at Van. "He didn't make the call."

"But somebody did." He glanced at the front door where the glass was scattered over the threshold. "Stay here while I check the back door and windows. Don't let anyone else in, and don't touch anything."

Harriet positioned herself so she could stop the curious from entering. She could see Wes better now. His wire-rimmed glasses lay a few feet away from where he was sprawled on the floor. One medic pushed up Wes's sleeve to start an IV drip, and the other examined the bloody wound on the side of his head.

Had Wes been attacked like Ivy?

Van returned, a confused expression on his face, and stood close enough to Harriet to talk without being overheard. "The back door is locked up tight, and there was no sign of a forced entry. In fact, there's a bar across the frame. Whoever was here didn't go out that way."

"Then the attacker must have come through the front door," Harriet mused. "Before I got here."

"When was that?"

"I couldn't say. No more than a few minutes."

"It's hardly been that long since the call came in. Besides, I had to unlock the dead bolt through the broken window to get inside."

"Which means anyone who left must have a key. Otherwise, the dead bolt couldn't have been locked." Harriet tilted her head as she stared at the landline. "I know it seems unlikely, but maybe he somehow hurt himself, called for help, and then fell again." Though that didn't make any sense. Why would he set the receiver down and move away from the phone without saying something?

"I might believe that if he were closer to the counter. But clear over here? I don't see it." Van knelt near Wes's feet. "Any thoughts on what happened?" he asked the medics.

"He has a nasty head wound, and he hasn't regained consciousness."

"Maybe he was trying to stop a robbery," the second medic chimed in. "Did you check the cash register?"

"It's locked," Van said, his tone frustrated. "Everything here is locked."

At that moment, Wes's eyelids fluttered. "Wake up, Wes," one of the medics said. "We're here to help you."

Wes responded with a groan. "Emma," he whispered.

"I'll call her," Van said. "I'm sure she'll meet you at the hospital."

Wes's eyes flickered open and landed on Harriet. He extended his arm toward her as if to reach for her hand. "The ghost knight."

His arm fell, and his eyes closed.

"He's blacked out again," one of the medics said. "His blood pressure is dropping. We need to get going."

While Harriet stood by, feeling helpless and worried, Van helped the medics move Wes onto the gurney and into the ambulance. One medic climbed in the back with Wes while the other got in the driver's seat. As it pulled away, Van asked the onlookers if they had seen anything suspicious. No one had, but one couple who'd been sitting at a window table inside the ice cream parlor across the street insisted no one had gone in or out of Uniquities in the last fifteen to twenty minutes.

"We wanted to stop in there," the woman explained, "so I kept an eye out in case Wes or Emma returned. They do sometimes. I had no idea Wes was already inside, or we'd have knocked on the door."

Van thanked them then encouraged the crowd to go on their way.

Like a few others, Harriet ignored that encouragement. Unlike the others, she stayed with Van while he called Emma. Then he took photos of the door he'd broken and the interior of the shop. He also took fingerprints around the doorknob and the cash register, even as he admitted to Harriet that it was probably a fruitless task. Anyone who had left prints could say they were a customer.

While Van gathered prints, Harriet examined the floor where Wes had fallen. Head wounds were notorious for bleeding profusely, and the wooden floorboards were stained a sickening shade of dark red.

"I don't understand," she said. "Someone was here with him and called emergency services. Why didn't that person say anything to the operator? Or at least try to stop the bleeding?"

"There's only one explanation I can think of." Van returned the fingerprinting equipment to its case. "Whoever called either hit Wes over the head on purpose or pushed him into that bookcase by accident. That person didn't want to be here when help arrived."

"I get that. But then why make the call in the first place?"

"Panic? Guilt?" Van gave her a world-weary smile. "Two attacks in less than a week. People aren't going to feel safe anymore."

"White Church Bay is still a safe place," Harriet assured him. "At least it will be once we find out who's behind these attacks. Though I don't know that we can assume the same person attacked Ivy and Wes."

"I pray there aren't two attackers," Van said. "One's enough. Especially one who's adept at not leaving clues."

"What about that scrap of fabric I found in Jiffy's mouth?" Harriet asked. "Did you learn anything from the crime lab about it?"

"I'm still waiting for the report. Could be a while before I get it."

"Did you take any photos of the fabric before you sent it to the lab?" Harriet asked, keeping her tone as nonchalant as possible.

Not that her ploy worked.

Van gave her a "that innocent act doesn't fool me" look. "As a matter of fact, I did."

"Could I see them?"

"Not unless you've traded your veterinarian license for a detective constable's badge."

Harriet snapped her fingers. "I knew I forgot something on my to-do list."

Unfortunately, she remembered all too well the clues she'd kept to herself—the reason why Ivy had gone to the cave in the first place, Fern's confession that she'd written the note, and Ivy's argument with Wes.

A pang of guilt struck Harriet's conscience. What if the argument had something to do with Wes's injury? Though how could it? Ivy certainly hadn't attacked him. But Wes could have lied to Harriet and Will. What if the argument had been about something besides a missing sculpture?

Harriet could keep Ivy's note a secret since she'd given her word, but Van needed to know about the argument.

"There's something I should tell you," she said, but Mr. Calabash appeared in the doorway and forestalled further conversation.

"Good evening, Detective Constable. Dr. Bailey," he greeted them. "I have a sheet of plywood to cover this doorway. We don't want anyone looting the place during the night, and Emma will have one less thing to worry about. I can put it up as soon as you're finished here."

"That's very neighborly," Harriet said. "I'm sure Wes and Emma will appreciate your thoughtfulness."

"So do I," Van said. Then he faced Harriet again. "You had something else to say?"

Harriet glanced at Mr. Calabash. She didn't want to say anything that might become small-town gossip in front of him. She smiled at Van. "Nothing that can't keep till later."

Van shrugged. "If you say so. There was something I wanted to ask you. That is, if you're not in too big a hurry."

"What is it?"

He took her by the arm and escorted her past Mr. Calabash and the lingering onlookers. He finally stopped on the other side of the Biscuit Bistro. But instead of saying anything, he removed his hat, ran his fingers through his short blond hair, and then tapped his hat against his leg.

Finally, Harriet prompted him. "You wanted to ask me something?"

"Yes. Yes, I did." His face flushed a crimson red. He took in a deep breath then practically exhaled his words. "Polly likes animals. Doesn't she?"

"Of course she does. It's what makes her so good at her job."

He twirled his hat in his hands. "A buddy of mine has tickets to a whale-watching expedition, but he can't go. He gave them to me, and I thought, since Polly likes animals, she might want to see the whales. They're minke whales. I'm not sure what those are, but if Polly wants to go, we could go together, and I'd find out. We might see dolphins too. The boat sails out of Whitby, and there's a lunch included. My buddy bought the VIP package, so we'd have the best seats. What do you think?"

Harriet's head reeled from the onslaught. Never had she known Van to say so much in so little time. "I think it sounds like fun."

"Does that mean you'll ask her?"

Harriet gaped at him. "You're asking me to ask Polly to go whale-watching with you?"

"Yes. I mean no." Van let out an exasperated sigh. "I'm doing this all wrong."

Harriet placed her hand on his arm. "You're doing fine. Now tell me, calmly and clearly, what you need from me."

"Before I ask Polly to go with me, I was wondering if you could find out if it's something she'd like to do. Because if it isn't, then there's no need for me to ask her."

"Oh, Van." Harriet dropped her hand to her side and took a moment to consider what to say. "Polly might enjoy it, or she might not. But here's what you need to know. A woman might agree to do something she'd rather not do because she wants to spend time with the man who asked her. On the other hand, she might say no to something she very much wants to do because she *doesn't* want to spend time with the man who asked her. Do you understand what I'm saying?"

Van slowly nodded, and he met Harriet's gaze. "I need to ask her myself, don't I?"

"Yes, you do."

"What if she turns me down?"

"What if she doesn't? You'll deal with it either way."

"Thanks, Harriet." Van settled his hat on his head and gave her a sheepish grin. "You're not going to tell Polly about this, are you?"

"My lips are sealed."

He returned to Uniquities.

Dear, sweet Van. He was smitten with Polly, but she didn't feel the same about him. "We're just friends," she'd told him. It was the same thing she told anyone who hoped to go beyond that status.

Harriet hugged herself against the chill of the North Sea as she trudged up the hill to her vehicle.

Love.

Was there any greater mystery? Her heart ached with the thought of it.

CHAPTER NINE

Harriet intended to order a pizza and go straight home, change her clothes, and curl up with her library book and Maxwell. But the same compulsion that led her to Uniquities now led her to the Whitby hospital. On the drive, she mulled over the attacker's actions. The same person who had caused Wes's injury had also likely called 999.

Who had done that? Why do that?

Van had suggested panic or guilt. Maybe a helping of both with a dollop of remorse thrown in for good measure. Did that mean Wes's injury was an accident? If so, why didn't the caller tell the emergency operator what had happened? Why not stay until the ambulance arrived?

The questions circled as Harriet entered the hospital's visiting area. She paused long enough to get her bearings, and spotted Will. He was probably making the rounds among the patients.

Harriet made a beeline for the vending machines. "What can I get you, Will? Coffee? Soda?"

Will turned in surprise and grinned. "Well, hello. I certainly wasn't expecting to see you this evening."

"Wes Brinley was attacked in his shop a short time ago. The ambulance brought him here, and I came too."

"Are you all right?" Concern softened his gaze.

"A little discombobulated. And puzzled." She told him what she knew about Van's investigation. "As far as I know, he's still at the shop."

"I heard the sirens when I was finishing up with the last person I visited." Will gestured at the vending machine. "I thought I'd grab something before going to the A&E to see if I was needed."

"I'm sure you will be, even if the Brinleys aren't members at White Church," Harriet said. "I wish I could go with you, but I'm sure Emma would find that strange."

"If you're not here for Emma or Wes, why did you come?"

The scene flashed through Harriet's mind, as vivid as if it were happening again in front of her. Wes, his eyelids fluttering as he tried to awaken, the medic calling his name. How Wes whispered Emma's name then reached for Harriet.

"The ghost knight."

The words had been slurred, almost unrecognizable. But Harriet had no doubt what Wes said before he blacked out again.

An uncontrollable shiver raced through her body, and Will touched her shoulder. "What is it?"

Harriet wrapped her arms around herself. "I'm here because of what Wes said." She closed her eyes and shivered again then chided herself for her foolishness. No ghost knight had attacked Ivy and Jiffy, then Wes. No ghost knight had mysteriously disappeared from the cave or from Uniquities.

"Tell me what he said," Will urged.

Harriet met his gaze, finding comfort and strength in the caring warmth of his eyes. Will was such a good man. A practical, compassionate man who had both feet solidly on the ground. He didn't believe in ghosts any more than Harriet did. And yet, there were so many unexplained phenomenas in the world. Could it be possible?

No. It could not.

"Harriet? What did Wes say?"

"He mentioned the ghost knight."

Will's eyes widened. "Meaning what?"

Harriet straightened her shoulders. Simply saying the words out loud had been enough for her to realize the ridiculousness of the notion that one of King Arthur's soldiers was wandering around the village and attacking people.

"I think he was telling us that was who attacked him." She was relieved her voice had returned to normal. "But that's not possible. So, who was it? And how did that person get out of the shop without being seen?"

"Those are good questions, and I'm sure Van is doing his best to find the answers."

Harriet averted her gaze. She agreed with Will. No doubt Van was doing the best he could, but he didn't have all the information that Harriet did. Neither did Will.

"I hate to say it, but Fern is lucky she has an alibi for the time of Ivy's attack," she said. Fern had been on the stage or with dozens of other people during the search. Though it was possible she could have assaulted Ivy before announcing her sister's absence, she couldn't have been the one who'd injured Jiffy. And she'd been wearing a lime-green dress that day, not a scarlet one so the fabric scrap didn't match.

"The sisters have their differences," Will said. "Everyone knows that, but even if Fern didn't have an alibi, I can't believe her capable of violence. Besides, why would she attack Wes?"

"Maybe because of the argument Wes and Ivy had before Ivy disappeared."

"But you told me Fern didn't witness the argument herself. Heidi Paxton told her about it."

"What if that's not true?"

When Will started to protest, Harriet held up a hand. "We know they argued," she said. "Wes admitted they did. But Fern seemed eager to shift any suspicion from her to him. Why would she do that? Why did I get the feeling that she was hiding something?"

"Because you made a promise to Skippy, and you want to keep it. But it's not your job to solve this mystery."

Maybe not. But she certainly felt a responsibility to do so. And not only for Jiffy's sake, but for Ivy, and now for Wes. One way to do that was to break her promise to Ivy and tell Van about the note. As soon as she had a chance, she needed to talk to Aunt Jinny about what she should do—preserve Ivy's confidence, or give Van information that might help him discover the ghost knight's identity.

A man and a woman in medical scrubs approached the vending machines, so Harriet and Will moved out of their way.

"You never said what you wanted," Harriet said with a smile, grateful for the interruption. She didn't like suspecting Fern or coming across to Will as a nosy busybody. At his puzzled expression, she tilted her head toward the vending machines. "Something to drink? A snack?"

"You're changing the subject."

Harriet drew her debit card from her purse. "My treat, remember?"

Will gave up. "Coffee and a package of mixed nuts sounds nice."

"You've got it."

Harriet made the purchases, including a bottle of water and a packet of toasted crackers for herself. Will retrieved his snacks and led the way to the visitors' desk, where he greeted the receptionist, an older woman with twinkling blue eyes behind fashionable glasses.

"You're having a relatively quiet night," Will said. "How's your grandson doing at university?"

A proud smile brightened the woman's face. "He's captain of the debate team this year. He'd have made a fine prime minister someday, but as much as he enjoys a spirited debate, he has no wish to be a politician. Too vicious an arena, he says."

"I can't say I blame him for that. What does he want to do instead?"

"Perhaps go into law, though he's not settled on any one thing yet."

"Please tell him I'm praying for him. And for you too, Maggie."

"I'll do that, Pastor Will, and thank you for doing so." She glanced toward Harriet. "You're the new veterinarian, aren't you? Old Doc Bailey's granddaughter?"

"Forgive my poor manners, ladies." Will introduced the two women, and they exchanged the usual pleasantries.

"I understand Wes Brinley is in A&E," Harriet said.

"I heard he was attacked in his own store." Maggie lowered her voice, even though no one else was around. "By a ghost, like Ivy Chapman and that poor dog."

"He was attacked, but not by a ghost," Will corrected.

"Perhaps not," she said doubtfully. "And yet, 'there are more things in heaven and earth, Horatio.' Isn't that what Hamlet said?"

"Yes, but I can assure you that Wes's attacker is a living, breathing person." Will's tone was polite but firm. "Do you know if Emma is here?"

"She arrived shortly after the ambulance."

"Would you mind letting her know I'm available, in case she or Wes need anything?"

"Happy to do so, Pastor." Maggie picked up her telephone. "I'll make the call right now."

Will nodded his thanks, and then he and Harriet settled in padded chairs that gave them a view of the doors leading to the Accidents and Emergencies department.

"Maggie isn't much of a churchgoer," he said as he took his seat. "But I never thought of her as the superstitious sort. All this talk of ghosts is ridiculous. Maybe I should preach a sermon on the topic."

Will's mention of a sermon caused Harriet's mind to leap to her own upcoming talk, which she'd all but forgotten in the excitement of the week. "How do you do it?" she asked.

"Do what?"

"Write a new sermon every week. The Whitby Women's Society asked me to speak at their next monthly luncheon, and I'm at a loss where to begin."

"What do they want you to talk about?"

"My move to Yorkshire. They seem to think it was a very courageous thing for me to do."

"I'd agree with that."

"Sometimes I would too. Other times…" She shrugged. "Maybe it wasn't so much courage as cowardice."

Will gave her a puzzled look. "Why would you say that? Cowards don't leave the comfort and safety of home to venture to faraway places. You left all that was familiar to you."

"It doesn't take courage to run away."

` "Is that what you were doing?"

"Maybe." She'd already confided the details of her broken engagement to Will, so there was no need to talk about it now.

A long silence followed, and then Will shifted in his seat to face her. "You were also running toward something," he said. "Not only a new house and a new country, but an entirely different place. You've embraced a new life with new customs and mannerisms and eccentricities. As wonderful as America sounds, I'm not sure I could give up all I know of Yorkshire and move to Connecticut. Despite the circumstances, you definitely did a very brave thing."

"That's kind of you." Harriet blinked as sudden tears burned the backs of her eyes. She turned away from Will but not soon enough.

"What is it, Harriet?" Concern filled Will's voice. "Do you regret coming here?"

"Not at all," she said quietly, thankful that her voice didn't crack. "I've fallen in love with Yorkshire, and I'm so grateful for Grandad's generosity. But lately, I've been having these unexpected bouts of homesickness. I find myself second-guessing my decision. Wondering if I made a mistake."

"And missing your family?"

"Immensely," she admitted with a small smile. "I doubt the women's society would be inspired by tales of my homesickness and regrets."

"Regrets?"

Harriet's eyes widened at the hurt in Will's tone when he uttered the word. Or had she imagined it?

"Not *regrets*. I'm not sorry I came, and I don't want to go back. I simply have these moments." She shook her head, unable to explain to him or anyone else—even herself—the mixed-up feelings she'd been experiencing. "Maybe that's one reason I'm fixated on finding the ghost knight. Trying to discover the identity of the mysterious attacker keeps my mind off this. I'm uncomfortable with feelings I don't understand."

Will nodded, his mouth pursed as if in deep thought, his gaze fixed on the double doors. Harriet doubted he even saw them. She'd noticed other times when he seemed to retreat into himself, staring off into the distance while working out something in his mind.

"Tuppence for your thoughts," she said gently, hoping he'd recall saying the same thing to her.

He pulled himself from his trance and chuckled. "All kinds of thoughts," he said, waving his hand in a circle around his temple. "The juxtaposition of courage and cowardice, of running away from something and toward something at the same time. Wondering if it matters how you apply any of that to your decision. Because here you are. You left home, and of course that's sad and hard and difficult. But you have a new home. All yours, to make of it whatever you want."

Harriet took in what he said, rolling the ideas around in her mind and sorting them out for herself.

"I can tell from your expression that I'm not making any sense. Forget all that."

Apparently, he'd mistaken her pondering for confusion.

"I'm thinking that I owe you a pound instead of tuppence. You've given me new ideas to consider in a more positive way."

"I'm glad." Will took out his phone and tapped the screen. "What you need for your talk is a unifying theme. The concept of home is one that encompasses everything else. Even if your listeners can't relate to your specific journey, they can relate to the idea of home." He flipped his screen around so she could read it. "Maybe this quote will help."

She read the words out loud. "'You can have more than one home. You can carry your roots with you and decide where they grow.'"

Intrigued, she took the phone from him and read the words again to herself, letting their simple yet encouraging message sink deep into her heart. Will, apparently sensing her need for brief solitude and reflection, didn't say anything. He merely sat beside her while giving her space to make the quote her own.

After a long silence, she thanked him. "I've never heard of Henning Mankell. Who is he?"

"A Swedish novelist who passed away about ten years ago. I haven't read any of his mystery novels, but I like that quote," he said. "Few of us live in the same house all of our lives, even if we don't move across an ocean. The point, though, is that you carry your American roots with you wherever you go. And you can plant them here, where you already have roots and where Baileys have lived for generations. You get to choose if you want to do that."

"Will you send that to me?" she asked as she returned the phone.

"Gladly." He tapped the screen a few times, texting her a screenshot of the quote.

When her phone dinged, she saved the screenshot to her photo library. She wanted to think about the quote some more, preferably while curled up in Grandad's favorite chair in his study with pen and paper in her hands so she could brainstorm what Will had characterized as juxtaposed themes—courage and cowardice, running to and running from—and how they related to her journey across the Atlantic. She envisioned a mind map around the word *home* and added an image of a woman carrying a bucketful of roots, confidently deciding where to plant them.

That decision had been made when she'd agreed to move to Yorkshire, but she hadn't arrived with the assurance that she could have more than one home.

Sometimes she yearned for the one she'd left behind and achingly missed her parents and friends. How could it be any other way when she'd grown up wrapped in so much love? It was completely natural.

She still didn't know exactly what she'd say to the women's group, but the mind map she envisioned would give her a place to begin.

"Thank you," she said again.

"Anytime."

The doors leading to the emergency department swung open, and Emma Brinley crossed the threshold into the waiting room. She appeared to be a few years younger than Wes, perhaps in her midthirties. Her strawberry blond hair hung in a long braid, and her eyes were red, as if she'd been crying. She had the same lanky build as Wes, though she seemed more comfortable in her body than Wes did in his. She moved with more grace than awkwardness as she saw Will and walked toward him.

Will stood, and Harriet rose beside him. "Should I leave the two of you alone?" she asked.

"Not yet," he said. "You'll want to know how Wes is doing."

He was right about that.

"Pastor Will," Emma declared, taking one of Will's hands in both of hers. "How good of you to come." She eyed Harriet. "I've seen you in Uniquities. The lady vet, right?"

"Emma," Will said, "this is Harriet Bailey. She was outside the shop when the ambulance arrived."

"Really?" Surprise flickered in Emma's eyes. "Do you know who did this awful thing?"

"I didn't see anyone," Harriet said. "Except Wes, of course. DC Worthington asked me to keep anyone else from coming in."

"Such an awful thing to have happened. I was home when the DC called. He told me he had to break the glass to get inside."

"The door was locked," Harriet said. "The dead bolt too."

"Strange," Emma said. "We seldom lock the door when we're there. Even when we're closed."

"Has Wes regained consciousness?" Will asked.

"Fortunately, yes." Emma hesitated, bending her head as if she needed a moment to compose herself. "The doctor said he's going to be okay after a day or two of rest, though I fear the blow has caused him to lose his senses."

"Why do you say that?" Will asked.

"He told the doctor he was attacked by a ghost knight." She shook her head in disbelief. "A medieval soldier wearing a scarlet tunic. It's ridiculous, of course, but he swears it's true. I think he's angry with me for not believing him."

"Ivy Chapman said the same," Harriet said. "Did you know she was attacked a few days ago?"

Emma waved her hand in a dismissive gesture. "I heard the talk about it, but I didn't believe it. She had to make up something after traipsing off like that when she was supposed to be at the pavilion overseeing the appraisal registrations and acting as the emcee. Had to save face."

The doors swung open again, and Van joined them. After a round of greetings, he addressed Emma. "I'll go back by the shop to be sure it's boarded up tight. I wish I knew how the assailant left there without being seen."

"Maybe I owe Wes an apology and he really did see a ghost," Emma said, her tone dripping with sarcasm.

"Would a ghost call 999?" Will asked.

"That's what I asked Wes," Emma said. "It's so like him to invent a story instead of admitting he's clumsy. I asked the doctor about it when we were alone. He said it's impossible to tell from the wound whether Wes was pushed or if he tripped over his own feet. I'm positive it was the latter."

Van glanced at Harriet, as if warning her not to reveal that it was highly unlikely that Wes made the emergency call. "Could be possible, I suppose."

They chatted a moment more. Then Emma invited Will to return to Wes's room with her. After the heavy doors closed behind them, Harriet and Van left the hospital together.

"It wasn't an accident," he said as they neared Harriet's vehicle. "You and I both know Wes didn't call 999, but that's a detail we need to keep to ourselves."

Heat rushed into Harriet's cheeks. "I already told Will." At the distraught expression on Van's face, she rushed to apologize. "I'm sorry. I'll text him right now and ask him to keep it to himself."

She pulled out her phone and quickly sent the text. Will immediately replied with a thumbs-up emoji, which she showed to the DC.

"At least I can trust him not to say anything," Van said, obviously annoyed at Harriet. "Can I count on you too? Don't even tell your aunt or Polly."

Harriet hid a smile at the way his voice softened when he mentioned Polly's name. "I promise."

She made another promise to herself. When she got home, she'd create a chart showing all the secrets she'd been told, who shared them, and who wasn't supposed to know. How else would she keep everything straight?

A shiver ran up her spine.

If she slipped, would the ghost knight come for her?

CHAPTER TEN

After closing the clinic at noon on Saturday, Harriet grabbed a bite to eat and worked on developing her talk for the Whitby Women's Society luncheon. First she wrote the quote Will had shown her across the top of a blank piece of paper. In the center of the page, she wrote *HOME* and drew a circle around it. Before long, the mind map she'd envisioned the evening before had taken shape, a spiderweb of interconnected thoughts and ideas that related to her central theme.

She highlighted the ones that resonated most strongly with her then wrote about them, stream-of-consciousness style, in a blank notebook. Though her intent was to focus on words of wisdom and anecdotes to pass along to her audience, the exercise soon became a therapeutic release of heartaches countered by prayers of gratitude for silver linings, blessings visible in hindsight, and the timeless reassurance of God's steadfast love.

Her Bible, peppered with highlighted passages and handwritten notes in the margin, lay open on the table to Psalm 84. Since she read the entire book of Psalms at least once or twice a year, she was confident she'd read this particular psalm many times before.

But today, when she'd done a search for the word *home* on a Bible website, the third verse had melted her heart. Happy tears dampened her cheeks as she added the scripture to her mind map and wrote it inside the front cover of the notebook.

Even the sparrow has found a home, and the swallow a nest for herself, where she may have her young—a place near your altar, Lord Almighty, my King and my God.

No matter where one might live, wasn't that the most important home of all—the one closest to God?

Harriet startled when the ornate wall clock chimed three o'clock. The initial appraisal of her umbrella stand was scheduled for that afternoon, and Ivy had urged her to be there in case it was selected for a video segment. She reluctantly closed her notebook and tidied her workspace. Though she still had much to do, her ideas now had substance and a direction.

Less than half an hour later, Harriet strolled past the stage to the veranda. As she had that first day Harriet met her, Ivy reigned behind the waist-high counter. A small cap attached to her hair with bobby pins covered her bandage.

"You're back," Harriet said warmly. "How are you feeling?"

"I'm fine now that I'm where I belong." Ivy's lilting tone lightened her words. "I assume you're here about your umbrella stand." She flipped through a box of ivory envelopes and handed Harriet one with her name on it. "The appraiser's report is in there, including contact information should you wish to arrange a meeting. If your item was chosen for a video segment, you'll find information on that too."

Harriet inwardly smiled as she carefully opened the envelope. Ivy had obviously repeated that little speech several times.

The envelope contained a matching ivory note card engraved with the words *Antique Festival* in black calligraphy on the front and a business card. The appraiser wasn't Heidi Paxton.

"What does it say?" Ivy asked. "I'm sure it has to be good news."

Harriet opened the card and deciphered the spidery handwriting. "It's a reproduction. The original is in the British Museum in London," she said as Ivy's eagerness melted into disappointment. "And is purported to have once belonged to Queen Victoria. It was a gift from a visiting Chinese diplomat who was under the impression that it rained every day in England. Hence, an umbrella stand."

Harriet thought the story was charming, but Ivy seemed less than impressed.

"Does it say how much the original is worth?" she asked.

"Its last valuation was estimated at 150,000 pounds. My reproduction is valued at, let me see, one-tenth of one percent of that."

"Only 150 pounds?" Ivy humphed and shook her head. "I don't suppose you received an invitation?"

Harriet picked up the envelope and gently squeezed the sides to show the interior to Ivy. "No video segment for me."

"I am sorry," Ivy said. "What do you want to do?"

"What are my choices?"

"Leave it on display until after the auction or take it home. You can also donate it to the auction if you wish. The reserve bid will be the appraisal amount. If it's not met, the stand will be returned to you."

"Let me think about it." The story about the Chinese diplomat intrigued her enough that she wasn't sure she wanted to part with the stand. Perhaps she could support the auction by buying something instead.

A sudden thought occurred to her. "What about Winston, Aunt Jinny's gargoyle?"

Ivy rolled her eyes and riffled through the envelopes again. "There's nothing for her yet. I still don't know why Jinny entered that monstrosity. She usually brings something delightful that is a boon to the spirit."

"Maybe she's hoping her 'trash' will be someone else's treasure."

"I believe I can safely say that hope is a vain one." Ivy glanced around as if to be sure no one could overhear them. "I heard you were at Uniquities when Wes Brinley was attacked yesterday. What happened?"

"I was outside the shop when Van and the ambulance arrived." Harriet told her about the locked doors but didn't mention the 999 call.

"Was he attacked by the ghost knight?" Ivy's voice had a now-do-you-believe-me undertone to it.

"That's what he says." Remembering that Van wanted the attacker to have a false sense of security, Harriet chose her next words carefully. "Another theory is that Wes fell on his own."

"Then why wouldn't he say so?" Ivy demanded. "He was attacked all right, just like I was. And not by any ghost either. I think it was Poppy Schofield."

Harriet blinked in surprise. "What makes you think that? Does she think Wes stole her coral rose cookie jar?"

"He's her number one suspect after he tried to cheat her out of a fair price for her Austrian porcelain platter." Ivy leaned closer. "She wouldn't want this to be common knowledge, but you have a way of getting to the truth of a matter, so I'll tell you this in the strictest confidence."

Great. Another secret to add to my list.

"Poppy ran into a spot of financial trouble not long ago. She placed the platter for sale at Uniquities on a commission basis and received a few hundred pounds for it. But last week she discovered that Wes sold it for much more than he said. Poppy demanded he give her the rest of the money he owed her, but he refused. He claimed that since she'd already signed the final payout forms, the transaction was closed."

Harriet's jaw dropped. "Wes did that?"

"Poppy says he did."

"Can't she take him to court? Report him to the Better Business Bureau?"

"The what?"

"Never mind. She must have some recourse. Doesn't Wes care about his reputation?"

"Apparently not." Ivy's blue eyes darkened, and her jaw clenched. Perhaps she was thinking about her own argument with Wes.

"I'm guessing he has some counterthreat," Ivy continued, "or Poppy would have made a public fuss about the matter. She told me because she'd heard that Wes and I also had our differences."

"You mean about the *Three Dogs at Night* sculpture?"

Ivy's mouth gaped open. "How do you know about that?"

"Wes told me."

Sudden anger flashed in Ivy's eyes. "I'm sure he didn't tell you the truth."

"He told me you were upset that he hadn't brought the sculpture to be appraised."

"Of course I was upset. A promise is a promise."

"He also said Emma brought it to you."

"Another one of his lies." Red spots appeared on Ivy's cheeks. "Then he had the gall to say I must have lost it. But I never would have. It was too—" She suddenly clapped her mouth shut and averted her gaze.

"Too what?" Harriet prodded, hoping Ivy would tell her more about her "dear friend."

A visitor approached the counter to ask about the antiques auction. "It's next Friday evening," Ivy told him. "The carnival packs up on Monday, and then we have a few days to get ready for our big event. The production company will use that time to edit the video segments, several of which will be highlighted during the auction. The extra days also give the owners of the appraised items more time to decide if they want to participate in the auction."

"That's quite a lot," Harriet observed.

"There's much to do to prepare for such a special evening." Ivy handed the visitor a pamphlet. "This provides an overview, and you can find even more information on our website. If you have any questions, contact me. If I'm not here, you can email me using the address on the back of the pamphlet."

During the interaction, Harriet couldn't help comparing Ivy's pleasant demeanor with her sister's more chaotic personality. She imagined Ivy was glad the visitor had interrupted their conversation, as it gave her a chance to compose herself.

When the visitor walked away, Harriet patiently waited for Ivy to answer her question about the sculpture. Ivy seemed just as determined to ignore her but eventually gave up.

"You Americans," she declared. "You have no manners. Brash and impudent, you are."

"I think you mean caring and concerned," Harriet countered. "Don't you want Van to find your attacker?"

"Of course I do."

"Then you can't keep secrets from him." She leaned closer and whispered, "He needs to know about the note and your argument with Wes."

"Wes is the one who's lying, not me." Ivy swiped at her cheek.

Once again, Harriet's heart ached for her. "Oh, Ivy. What aren't you telling me?"

"None of your business. Run along now. I've work to do."

Harriet tucked the appraisal information into her bag and wandered toward the food booths. She stopped by the Biscuit Bistro booth where Poppy was boxing a selection of cookies for a young mom and her two children. When it was Harriet's turn, she chose half a dozen rock cakes, a kind of raisin cookie, for her and Will to take with them on their trip to Richmond tomorrow afternoon.

"It looks like you're doing a thriving business," Harriet said. "No surprise when you make such delicious cookies. I mean biscuits."

"You can call them cookies," Poppy said kindly. "We get enough American tourists in the summer that I know their lingo."

Harriet smiled. "I was wondering if you ever found out who took your coral rose cookie jar."

"I have my suspicions but not an iota of proof. It bothers me that what started out as silly practical jokes has turned to thievery."

"I suppose you heard what happened to Wes Brinley."

"Indeed I did. I left a message for Detective Constable Worthington earlier today about arranging a meeting with the shop owners on our street. Whoever is causing all this trouble needs to be stopped before something truly horrible happens."

"I imagine Wes already feels like something horrible happened to him."

"He'll get over a bump on the head soon enough," Poppy said with little pity.

"Forgive me for saying so, but you don't seem to like Wes very much."

"I certainly don't wish him ill." Poppy worked her jaw as though deciding what to tell Harriet. "He's not a friend though."

Harriet waited a couple of beats, but apparently Poppy had said all she was going to say. Harriet, however, wasn't ready to give up yet. She wanted to hear Poppy's side of the story Ivy had told her without coming right out and asking about it.

"I only met Wes a couple of days ago," Harriet said, keeping her tone casual. "Though I've been to Uniquities a time or two. They carry such unusual items."

"That's their specialty."

"I can't help wondering what the connection is between him and Ivy. Who do you suppose is pretending to be this ghost knight who attacked them?"

Suddenly Poppy straightened her shoulders, and her tone lost all its prior friendliness. "Surely you don't suspect me."

"Suspect you?" Harriet hoped she sounded shocked, though from Poppy's expression, she might have failed at that. "I never would." Which was true. Ivy was the one who'd pointed a finger at Poppy.

"You may as well take your suspicions elsewhere," Poppy said. "I was here in this booth when Ivy was attacked, and I was in Whitby yesterday evening. An old school chum lives there, and we went to a movie. I can give you her number if you wish."

"There's no need for that," Harriet assured Poppy, her cheeks warm from embarrassment.

"Are you certain?" Poppy's tone was decidedly icy.

"Please believe me. I didn't mean to upset you. It's only that someone mentioned you and Wes were at odds with each other. I don't need to talk to your friend or anyone else to know you didn't hurt him."

Poppy didn't seem entirely mollified, but at least steam no longer came out of her ears.

"Will you forgive me?" Harriet asked, and this time she didn't have to pretend to be sincere. She truly didn't want Poppy upset with her.

"Of course I will." Poppy bagged up a triangular shortbread cookie dusted with icing sugar and handed it to Harriet. "This is called a petticoat tail. The recipe was handed down from my great-grandmother, and it's a famous family secret. I only bake them on special occasions."

Harriet meekly accepted the treat. "You're very kind. Thank you."

"Just tell whoever pointed the finger at me that when I want to confront Wes, it won't be as a ghost or a knight or any such silliness. I won't even ask you who spoke such nonsense." She froze then tilted her head in thought. "By chance, have you spoken to Heidi Paxton?"

Startled by the mention of the appraiser's name, Harriet shook her head. "We've never met. Should I?"

"I don't want to point fingers in the wrong direction either," Poppy said. "But she and Wes were exchanging rather unpleasant words the other day."

How odd. Heidi was the one who'd told Fern that Wes and Ivy had argued—that is, if Fern was telling the truth. And now Poppy said that Heidi and Wes also had an argument? Was that a coincidence or a clue?

"When was this?" she asked.

"The same day Ivy was attacked. After all the hubbub from the search and rescue helicopter flying by and then taking off again, I closed my booth to watch the amateur talent show. Naturally, everyone was talking about Ivy and Jiffy and hoping they'd be okay. But Heidi and Wes were off to one side, and neither one looked happy."

"Do you know what the argument was about?"

"I'm not one to eavesdrop. Neither do I have any interest in getting involved with Wes Brinley's drama."

Another customer arrived, so Harriet thanked Poppy again for the cookies and headed toward the parking lot, her mind in a muddle.

Ivy accused Poppy, and Poppy accused Heidi. Who would Heidi accuse? Fern?

If only Harriet could sort out the tangle of lies and secrets. But the task seemed increasingly impossible. And given that two people in the thick of it had already been attacked, maybe even dangerous.

CHAPTER ELEVEN

Harriet drove home after church on Sunday morning to take care of Maxwell and Charlie, change her clothes, and fix a lunch for her and Will to enjoy on their drive to Richmond.

"Peanut butter and jelly sandwiches sound good, don't they, Maxwell?" Harriet said to the dachshund. "We're researching the legend of the lost drummer boy after all."

Maxwell yipped as if in agreement then pawed the air. Harriet chuckled, placed a bit of peanut butter on a dog biscuit, and gave it to him.

Harriet placed the sandwiches, made with slices of hearty grain bread and cut in triangles, into an insulated tote along with carrot sticks, apple slices, the rock cakes she'd bought the day before from Poppy, and bottles of water. The light lunch was meant to stave off hunger pangs while they saw the sights. Then they would enjoy a local meal before returning to White Church Bay.

When the tote was packed and zipped, Harriet squatted in front of Maxwell. "Will and I will be gone for a few hours. But we'll have playtime when I get back. Until then, let's take this thing off, okay?"

Maxwell pushed his nose beneath Harriet's folded arms, and she hugged his long body then removed the wheeled prosthesis. She settled Maxwell in his bed with another biscuit slathered in peanut butter.

She finished tidying the kitchen just as the front doorbell rang. "That should be Will," she said, grabbing the tote and giving Maxwell one more pat.

She went through the hallway between the stairs and the study to reach the front entrance.

When she opened the door, Will greeted her with a warm smile. "Let me take that," he said, reaching for the tote. "You ready to go?"

"Ready and excited." She retrieved a tan hip-length fleece-lined jacket from the nearby hall tree, and they set out for the drive to Richmond in Will's Picanto.

Once they were on the main road, Harriet doled out the sandwiches, veggies, and rock cakes. The time sped by as she enjoyed Will's company.

As they neared the historic market town, Richmond Castle came into view. It towered over the village below and the River Swale, which curved south of the grounds. Harriet opened a travel guide she'd found in Grandad's library and scanned the castle's listing.

"The origins date to 1071," she said. "I can hardly fathom it."

"That's only a couple of years after William the Conqueror swept through Yorkshire," Will explained. "After he conquered these lands, he gave them to his buddies."

"In this case, Alan Rufus of Brittany. But the keep—" She peered through the windshield at the honey-colored sandstone castle. "Is that what I'm seeing? That's the keep?"

"Sure is," Will said, chuckling, apparently at her excitement. "Also known as a fortified tower."

"I'll never get used to how old things are here. Thousand-year-old castles. Roman ruins." Harriet released a deep, awe-filled sigh. "It's all so fascinating."

"What were you saying about the keep?"

As difficult as it was to pull herself away from the sight of the high tower overlooking the town, Harriet returned to the guide. "It was built in the late 1100s. Towers were added to the castle and so was a barbican. What's a barbican?"

"It's a kind of fortified gateway into the castle grounds. An enemy would have to fight his way through the barbican or scale the outer walls if he wanted to get inside."

While Will followed the navigational app's directions to a car park central to the area they planned to explore, Harriet shared more of the castle's history, including how it was used as the Non-Combatant Corps base during World War I. The military unit was made up of conscientious objectors who provided physical labor both in Britain and overseas.

Harriet closed the guidebook. "We're not going to have time to tour the castle today, are we?"

"I doubt it." Will pulled into an open spot and turned off the ignition. "Though there's no reason we can't come back again if you want to."

Harriet's stomach fluttered, and she pushed the sensation away. As much as she enjoyed Will's company, she wasn't ready for flutters. Only friendship mattered in this season of her life.

They followed the walking tour info that Will had found online to the ruins of Easby Abbey. The soldiers who'd found the tunnel entrance at the castle expected it to lead to the abbey, which was built about the same time as the keep. In the 1530s, King Henry VIII had rid his kingdom of its monasteries because Pope Clement VII opposed his wish to divorce Catherine of Aragon. The abbey was abandoned during that purge.

Harriet gazed up at the stone walls, the glassless window frames, and the remains of the gatehouse, imagining how magnificent the abbey must have been several hundred years ago. "What do you suppose life was like for the monks who lived here?"

"For a time, peaceful," Will said. "I believe they raised sheep. And they were called canons instead of monks."

After exploring the grounds and visiting nearby St. Agatha's Church, Harriet and Will meandered along the narrow path bordered by the River Swale on one side and woods on the other. They were walking in the opposite direction as the soldiers and the boy—from the abbey to the castle instead of from the castle to the abbey.

Eventually, at a fork in the path, they reached the drummer boy's memorial.

A slab of rock stood upright on a stone base that held a plaque titled THE DRUMMER BOY'S STONE. To the left of the inscription was a drawing of a drummer boy wearing a weathered red uniform.

Will read the words aloud. "'According to legend, this stone marks the spot where the Richmond drummer boy reached in the tunnel supposed to lead from Richmond Market Place to Easby Abbey. Here, the sound of his drumming ceased, and he was never seen again.'" He paused. "Whoever wrote that could probably use a grammar lesson."

A soft breeze brushed Harriet's cheek, causing her to shiver. "What do you suppose actually happened to the child?" she asked, her tone as quietly respectful as if they were standing beside a grave. Perhaps they were.

"It would have been dark in the tunnel." Will gazed back in the direction of the abbey then toward Richmond Castle, though neither could be seen through the trees. "If he reached this spot, he'd already gone quite a way. Maybe he got trapped."

"I can't imagine how frightened he must have been."

They stood in silence for a few more moments then followed the path to the bridge beside the waterfall. The cold waters of the River Swale cascaded over hidden rocks on its eastern journey to the North Sea.

The sparkling beauty of the waterfall's short drop gave Harriet a needed respite from the mournful gravity that had surrounded her since they'd been at the stone. Her spirits lightened as she breathed in the fresh scents of cleansing waters and autumn crisp breezes.

"It's so tranquil," she murmured. "As if we're at one of those thin places I've read about." She bit her lip. What if Will didn't know what she was talking about, and she sounded silly trying to describe it?

"As if heaven were close," he said, surprising her that he did know. "Almost touchable."

"Thank you for bringing me here. I wasn't expecting to feel this emotional about something that happened in the days of King Arthur."

"Who is himself a legend," Will reminded her. "Even if it was possible for the drummer boy to talk to one of Arthur's knights, how would the soldiers have known what they said to one another? They were aboveground, following the drumbeats. All they knew was that the drumming stopped."

"I thought of that," Harriet admitted. "But I suppose it's one of those impossible legends that one wants to be true. I'd much rather the little boy fell asleep with King Arthur's knights than to…" She let the words trail off.

"Sounds to me like you need a hot cuppa."

"Tea." Harriet lifted her lips into a slight smile. "The English answer for all one's ailments."

"I'm often amazed at how true that is," Will said. "Let's go find that pub."

The path led them back to the car park, but they went beyond it to the village's main cobbled square. A drummer boy banner hung in front of a museum, related souvenirs could be seen in a few of the shop windows, and a painted, life-size statue stood in front of a slender tree.

Harriet paused in front of a bookstore window to get a closer look at a display featuring various editions of *Alice's Adventures in Wonderland* and related toys and games.

"Lewis Carroll attended grammar school here in Richmond," Will said. "The poor man gets overshadowed by the legend, but I can't help wondering if it inspired him. He had to know the story."

Harriet quickly connected the dots. "Because Alice fell down a rabbit hole and had trouble finding her way out again."

"Perhaps the drummer boy was an unnamed guest at the Mad Hatter's tea party," he teased. He gestured toward the opposite corner. The faded sign over the angled doorway depicted an old-fashioned drum. "There's the Camelot Pub. Shall we?"

They crossed the cobbled square, and Will held the heavy door open for Harriet to precede him into the foyer. At this time of day, a couple hours before the dinner rush, there were few diners.

An open coat closet lined one wall while a padded bench lined the other. An enormous print of the lost drummer boy statue hung in an ornate wooden frame with gilt edging above the bench. Two other paintings, slightly smaller than that of the statue, flanked the central frame.

The first showed an attractive illustrated map of the walking path from the castle entrance to Easby Abbey. Soldiers dressed in medieval uniforms marched single file along the section of the path before the fork where the memorial stone was located.

A portion of the illustration was a cutaway of the tunnel itself, drawn below the grass, and included the cavern. The nameless boy, his drum strapped across his shoulder, stood beside a knight clad in a scarlet tunic. Other knights slept on the ground around them.

The other painting was an enlarged and more detailed illustration of the underground cavern shown in the opposite one. Harriet stepped closer to get a better look, and gasped. The scarlet tunic worn by the knight who stood beside the drummer boy had gold embroidery on the sleeve and hem that closely resembled the pattern she'd seen on the fabric scrap.

Unless her mind was playing tricks on her.

If only she'd been able to talk Van into showing her a photo of the scrap. That thought sparked an idea. She couldn't see a photo of the scrap, but she could show Van a photo of this knight's uniform.

She pulled out her phone, but Will placed his hand on hers. "Hang on." He pointed to a banner above the frames. It read: No PHOTOGRAPHS, PLEASE. PRINTS AVAILABLE AT THE COUNTER.

"This fabric resembles the scrap I took from Jiffy's mouth. See the gold thread and this design?" Her voice grew more excited. "There *is* a connection between the attacker and the drummer boy."

Will bent closer to peer at the image. Harriet almost expected him to pull out a magnifying glass.

"We need to see those prints," she urged.

Will led the way to the counter, where they found copies of the individual paintings plus collages ranging in size from postcards to posters. A small rack also held an assortment of drummer boy-related keychains and magnets.

Harriet selected a large print of the cavern image and studied it. "The detail of the embroidery is large enough on this one for me to show Van. He can compare it with the fabric he took as evidence."

Will tapped a print of the walking path illustration. "This tunnel has nothing to do with the cave by the festival grounds," he said, "and this legend has nothing to do with White Church Bay. What's the connection?"

"That's what we need to figure out," Harriet answered. "I'm going to get those too. I might as well have a set." She chose prints of the other two paintings and laid all three on the counter while she dug her wallet from her bag.

As she paid for her purchases, the hostess invited them to sit wherever they wished. Will led the way to a window table that overlooked an interior courtyard with seating areas and a wooden statue of the lost drummer boy. The paneled walls between the courtyard windows were decorated with an assortment of modern photographs showing individuals dressed as knights and soldiers, kings and nobility, peasants and minstrels. The outfits ranged from simple homespun garb to elaborate costumes that appeared to be made of luxurious fabrics and furs.

Instead of sitting, Harriet and Will scanned the photographs.

"What's this all about?" Harriet asked.

"I don't know, but it looks like fun."

Harriet pointed to a man dressed in a burgundy and gold tunic with a matching coat bordered in brown fur. He wore a golden crown inset with huge red, blue, and green gemstones. "He reminds me of Henry VIII before he gained so much weight. Would you wear something like that?"

"I might." Will tapped a photo of a man wearing a plain brown robe with a rope sash and a large cross necklace. "Though this one is more my style."

"I'm glad that's not the style you have to wear today."

"Me too. What about you? Which of these costumes would you wear?"

As Harriet tried to decide, a waitress approached with glasses of water and menus. After welcoming them to the pub, she introduced herself as Tara. "Are you looking for your photos?"

"No," Will said. "We're only curious about them. Can you tell us what they're for?"

"They're all medieval reenactors," Tara explained. "We had the privilege of hosting a medieval fair here in Richmond a few years ago. That's when most of these snaps were taken, though sometimes a reenactor will bring a new one from a more recent fair. They're held throughout the country every summer."

"I've heard of those fairs but never attended one," Will said. "The reenactors can be quite passionate about their roles, can't they?"

"Indeed they can," Tara agreed. "A few of the groups have a hierarchy, just as those in ancient times."

"What do you mean, a hierarchy?" Harriet asked.

Tara's smile widened, and her eyes sparkled. "You're an American, aren't you? Here for holiday?"

"Here to stay," Harriet said with a smile. She averted her gaze as the casual words settled into her heart with more impact than she would have expected. As if they held a truth she'd always known but had been reluctant to embrace.

When she looked up again, Will gave her a reassuring smile, as though he knew what she was feeling without her having to put it into words.

"This is my home now," she said to Tara. "Not here in Richmond, but on a farm outside White Church Bay."

Tara stared at her with renewed interest. "Would you be the new lady vet we've heard tell of?"

"Guilty." Harriet pronounced the word with hesitation. "How did you know?"

Will chuckled. "Word gets around. I imagine everyone in Yorkshire has heard of you by now."

"The way folks like to talk, that is sure to be true," Tara added. "My cousin's wife—his name is Bob Stipple and her name is Agnes. She used to be Agnes Grey, like the title character in the Anne Brontë novel. Have you read that?"

"My grandfather gave me his copy when I came to visit one summer," Harriet replied. "I felt a kinship with Anne. After reading her novel, I believe she loved animals as much as I do."

"Our Agnes loves animals too. That's why when she went to visit her sister, Betsy Gant, she heard tell of you. Betsy and her husband raise a small herd of sheep and an even smaller herd of cattle on their farm outside White Church Bay. You went to see them a month or so ago for one of their ewes who was in a bad way."

"That's right. Betsy gave me a casserole to take home. It was delicious."

"She liked you very much. Agnes told us all about it at Sunday dinner shortly thereafter."

"Tara," a booming voice called from the counter. A large man holding a spatula and wearing a chef's coat scowled at her. "Those good folks came in here because they're hungry, not to hear you go on like you do."

"In a minute," Tara called back. "They haven't given me their orders yet."

"Well, they probably can't get a word in edgewise," the chef retorted.

"We're still trying to decide," Will said, raising his voice slightly. "Everything sounds delicious."

"Take your time," the cook said. "As long as she's not bothering you."

"Not at all," Harriet assured him. Then she lowered her voice. "I hope we haven't gotten you in trouble, Tara."

"Don't worry about me," Tara said. "That's Bob's third cousin twice removed on his mother's side, which means we're cousins too, though I can never remember exactly how. He can't fire me without causing a family ruckus. Truth be told, I would never give him cause to do so, and he wouldn't let me go if I did. No one else keeps the kitchen as tidy as I do." She poised her pen over her pad and gave them an expectant look. "What would you like? Today's special is shepherd's pie."

"Sounds fine to me," Will said. "Harriet?"

"Make that two, please." They also selected an assorted bread basket and fizzy drinks, as Will called soda, from the menu.

After Tara wrote down their order, she retrieved the menus and returned to the kitchen.

"I guess the Gants were happy with how you treated their animals," Will said as they took their seats.

"I'm surprised," Harriet admitted. "Betsy was hospitable and warm, but her husband seemed to doubt everything I said."

"Did the ewe survive and thrive?" Will grinned at his rhyme, and Harriet responded with a grin of her own.

"She most certainly did."

"Results like that will win over the doubtingest doubter. The Gants' livestock is their livelihood. They want a vet who cares about their animals as much as they do."

Harriet beamed with appreciation, both for Will's affirmation and for the sweet gift God had bestowed on her. Though she hadn't seriously considered packing up all her earthy goods to return to Connecticut, she was grateful for the unexpected—albeit roundabout way—that God had shown her that she was needed here. Her career had never been "just a job" to her. Thanks to the experience Grandad had given her whenever she came for a visit, and to his influence, providing care to animals was her ministry. It was why she could get up in the middle of the night to answer an emergency call then keep all the next day's appointments. The reason she wouldn't give up on any animal.

She mentally whispered a prayer of thanks, sipped her water, and then spread the prints she'd purchased in the middle of the table.

"This is what I want to show Van." She pointed to the gold embroidery at the knight's wrist. "He can compare it to the fabric that Jiffy tore from the attacker."

Will picked up the print and examined it. "You say the fabric is the same color as the one in this photo?"

"Maybe not exactly, but it's close. Perhaps whoever attacked Ivy is one of these medieval reenactors." Harriet waved her hand at the wall of photos. "He could have seen this print and modeled his costume after it."

"Interesting theory. Plausible, even." Will shifted in his chair to study the photographs. Harriet followed his gaze. "Some of these photos have been up here for years. See the dates?" He pointed to the photographs in the center of the wall. "The oldest ones date back to the 1990s."

"That's nice in this day of camera phones," Harriet said. "These people go to the trouble to have their photos printed for the wall. They must consider it an honor."

"Tara started to say something about a hierarchy before she got sidetracked about the Gants' ewe. I wonder what she meant by that."

Harriet glanced toward the bar. "She's bringing our drinks. We can ask her."

"As long as Cousin Cook doesn't get annoyed," Will said with a grin.

Tara placed their glasses on the table, careful to avoid the prints.

"We were wondering about the photos," Harriet said. "I mean the ones on the walls. Can anyone put their picture there?"

"As long as they can find a spot."

"You said something about a hierarchy earlier," Will said. "What did you mean by that?"

"If the two of you go to this particular troupe's medieval fair," Tara explained, "the regulars would welcome you with open arms, no matter what costumes you were wearing. But once you join the 'court'"—she made air quotes—"you start out as a commoner. They have games, tests, and competitions so you can earn points, and that's how you move up in the ranks. Eventually, if you get enough points, you can be a knight or even royalty."

"What about king?" Will asked.

Tara hugged her tray to her chest. "There's only one of those, and you must have reached royalty status to be selected. That's because the royalty are the ones who organize the fairs. The king and queen cochair the committee."

"What a fun blend of the historical and contemporary." Harriet tapped the knight in the print she'd purchased. "Have you ever seen anyone with a costume like this one?"

"It's a popular costume. After all, who doesn't want to be the knight who spoke to the drummer boy?" Tara pointed to a wall between two other windows where a family enjoyed their meals. "We keep most of the snaps of the knights there, as a kind of collection."

A bell rang, and Tara glanced toward the bar. "That's your order. I'll be right back."

"We'll have to wait until they're done eating to look at the wall," Will said.

"Eat slow," Harriet said with a chuckle as she moved her prints off the table.

As they enjoyed the hearty casserole, made with ground lamb and cheesy mashed potatoes, their conversation drifted from the drummer boy and the ghost knight attacks to other topics. They never seemed to run out of conversation, though it didn't matter when they did. Their silences were companionable, never awkward. In the past few months, Will had become a good and trusted friend. It was nice to enjoy such a comfortable relationship with a member of the opposite sex. No expectations. No stomach somersaults.

Okay, maybe a few somersaults. But mostly comfortable.

For dessert, they selected red velvet cupcakes decorated like drums at Tara's recommendation. Since the family had left by that time, Will suggested they check out the wall. As Tara had said, most of the photographs were of different individuals dressed up as the knight who stood next to the drummer boy in the cavern.

The costumes weren't identical. Unless the color was off in the film processing, the shades of red weren't consistent. Neither was the pattern of the gold embroidery on the sleeve and hem of the tunic the same on any two costumes.

"I think this is the one most like the scrap I saw," Harriet said, pointing to a picture of a man with wavy brown hair. "And maybe this one." She tapped a second one.

"You're sure about this one?" Will used his knuckle to indicate the first photo.

Something in the tone of his voice caught Harriet's attention. "As sure as I can be. Why?"

Will pressed his lips together, as if he didn't want to answer her.

"Will? What is it?"

All his levity was gone. "I know him."

"Oh." Harriet paused. "Who is he?"

"His name is Andrew Ellsworth. He owns a discount antique store." Will released a heavy sigh and held Harriet's gaze. "He and Wes are rivals. And not friendly ones."

CHAPTER TWELVE

Monday became a busier day than Harriet had expected when a golden retriever swallowed a small rubber ball and needed emergency surgery. To complicate matters, the dog was three weeks pregnant.

When the clinic closed at four, Harriet hurried to change into dark trousers and a turquoise sweater. She freshened her makeup then rushed to the Beast. Even so, it was a few minutes past five when she arrived at White Church.

Will waited for her outside the rectory's entrance, so she didn't bother to park.

"Tough day?" he asked as he settled into the passenger seat. "I heard about Nugget. How is she?"

When Harriet first arrived in Yorkshire, she was surprised at how quickly news sailed through the air from Cobble Hill Farm to the village. But not anymore. Now, it seemed that other people knew what happened at the clinic almost before she did.

"The operation was a success, and the puppies should be okay. But Nugget is spending a quiet night at the clinic, so I can't be gone too long." She wrestled with the gear shift to get the transmission into first and headed for the upper-level car park. Automobiles weren't allowed on the narrow street where Andrew Ellsworth's discount antique store was located.

"If you want, we can put off our visit until tomorrow," Will offered.

"If Andrew is the ghost knight, we need to know sooner rather than later." *Before he attacks Wes again. Or anyone else.* "Besides, Aunt Jinny is dog-sitting for me. She'll keep an eye on Nugget until I return."

"I promised Sarah Jane I'd pray for her. She loves that dog."

"A girl's first love should be her dog," Harriet said. "She called me as soon as she got home from school. I told her to call me again before her bedtime and I'd give her an update."

"That's why your clients think so highly of you. You go above and beyond, like Old Doc Bailey." He smiled at her, and Harriet grinned back at him before she focused her attention on the road.

"Will Andrew's store still be open?"

"No, but he said he'd wait for me."

"Does he know I'm coming?"

"I knew I forgot to tell him something," Will teased.

"Pastor Will, I'm shocked."

They both laughed, which eased the dread that had begun squeezing Harriet's stomach the moment she'd left her house. On the way back from Richmond yesterday, she and Will had decided it wasn't fair to Andrew to tell Van about the photograph they'd seen. It proved nothing when there were so many others with similar costumes. It certainly didn't prove that Andrew had attacked Ivy or Wes. Neither did the rivalry between the two business owners.

Will said the antagonism had been going on since Wes and Andrew were in secondary school. Neither had physically attacked the other before, not even when they were hotheaded teens. Why would that change now? Harriet and Will's best course of action was to first talk to Andrew and see what he had to say. Then they would contact Van if it seemed necessary.

Andrew's store, a two-story sandstone building sandwiched between a pharmacy and a narrow alley, boasted two large display windows on either side of a cobalt blue door. The frames around the windows and the eaves were painted the same color.

As Will had expected, the front door was locked. They walked through the alley, past an old farm wagon, an iron bed frame, and even a rusted plow to the back door. A moment or two after Will knocked, the door was opened by a man with wavy brown hair.

Harriet immediately recognized the medieval reenactor from the photo. Will made the introductions, then Andrew ushered them to a small break room. They settled around a wooden table with bottles of water and a package of store-bought biscuits.

"Now, Pastor," Andrew said, apparently not interested in engaging in polite pleasantries. "Tell me what this is all about. I figured you wanted a donation to the church fund, but you don't need the lady vet with you for something like that."

"I leave the financial matters to God," Will said. "I suppose you know what happened to Ivy Chapman and Wes Brinley."

At the mention of Wes's name, Andrew snorted. "Sounds to me like Wes angered the wrong person. It was bound to happen sooner or later."

"You don't like him very much, do you?" Harriet asked.

"I'm sure Pastor Will already told you that Wes and I don't get along. He and his cousin strut around this town with their noses in the air, as if they're better than the rest of us. Their business might cater to a wealthier clientele than my little enterprise, but at least I never cheat people."

"Are you saying Wes does?" Will's eyes narrowed as he tilted his head. "That's a serious allegation, Andrew. Do you have proof?"

"He's good at covering his tracks."

Perhaps not as good as he thinks, Harriet mused to herself. Now she wished she'd told Will what Poppy had said about Wes undervaluing an item she'd placed on consignment at Uniquities.

Will leaned back in his chair. "Harriet and I were at the Camelot Pub in Richmond yesterday. I had no idea you were involved in medieval reenactments."

"It's a hobby. Saw my picture on the wall, did you?"

"We did."

Harriet placed the print of the cavern painting in front of Andrew and pointed at the knight standing by the drummer boy. "Whoever attacked Ivy and Wes wore a medieval costume similar to this one."

"Similar to the one you're wearing in the snap at the pub," Will added.

Andrew's eyes rounded. "You think *I* attacked them? Why would I do that?"

Will didn't answer, so Harriet didn't either. Though she had to admit that if Andrew was the ghost knight, he was a very good actor. He seemed genuinely shocked to be accused of the attacks.

"Miss Ivy used to babysit me. Even when I was a teen and my mum worked nights, I'd stay at her house." He stared at the floor and shook his head, visibly upset. A moment later, he glared at Will. "I wouldn't have passed math if it wasn't for Miss Ivy. She's a whiz at calculations and theories. I'd never hurt her." His voice hardened. "Never."

"What about Wes?" Will asked, his voice quiet.

"Him either. We have our differences. Everyone in the village knows that. But I have no intention of going to jail on an assault charge. Wes Brinley isn't worth me being locked up. That wouldn't exactly help my business, would it?"

"I believe you, Andrew," Will said. "Still, it would ease my mind to know where you were during the attacks."

"I need an alibi?"

Will raised his eyebrows, a kind but firm indication that he expected Andrew to answer.

"When Miss Ivy was attacked, I was here at the store waiting on customers, a few locals and a few out-of-towners. Ask Jane Birtwhistle if you don't believe me. She was shopping for a birthday gift when we heard the news."

Harriet inwardly smiled at the mention of the retired school-teacher. Notorious for providing a home for any stray cat that wandered past her cottage, she'd been one of Harriet's first clients in White Church Bay.

"What about the evening Wes was attacked?" Will asked.

Andrew took a long drink from his water bottle. "My wife left that day to visit her mum in Birmingham. If I'd known I would need an alibi, I'd have closed the store and gone with her."

"Mr. Ellsworth—" Harriet began.

"Please, call me Andrew. Everybody does."

"Okay, Andrew. I know this may seem strange, but could I see your costume?"

"Sure," he said, scooting his chair back and standing. "We have a couple of storage rooms upstairs. All my reenactment regalia is up there, plus various things belonging to our troupe. I'll go get it."

He was gone a few moments then returned with a bound album rather than the costume. "It's not up there," he said, as if stunned. "I thought my missus picked it up from the dry cleaner before she left, but maybe she forgot."

"Maybe she took it to your house," Harriet suggested.

"I tried calling her to see, but she didn't answer." Andrew shifted his gaze between Harriet and Will. "Why do I feel like I'm under suspicion if you don't see my costume?"

"I don't mean to make you feel that way," Harriet said. "I simply want to find out what happened in the cave. Not only was Ivy attacked, but so was Jiffy, the search and rescue dog who found her."

"I heard about that too. Believe me, I want the lowlife snake found and brought to justice. But the snake isn't me." Andrew laid the album on the table. "My wife made this scrapbook. You'll see I'm not the only reenactor who dresses up like one of King Arthur's knights."

He opened the cover and flipped past the first few pages. The page he landed on had a medieval-themed background with a faded castle surrounded by a moat and knights mounted on regal horses. Photos and stickers decorated the page, while pertinent info was written in a bold calligraphy font.

"Here I am," he said, pointing to the central photo on the page. "This is the first time I wore that costume, the day I was knighted."

The album spanned a couple of years, each section clearly labeled with the name of the fair, the place, and the date. Andrew flipped through the pages, pausing to point out photographs of his knighting ceremony and identifying individuals he thought Will might know.

Most of the photographs were posed—Andrew with other knights, Andrew with the king and queen of the fair, Andrew with his page. Others were snapshots of the reenactors participating in a variety of games or feasting on giant turkey legs.

Harriet thought she recognized a few of the people who had also posted their pictures on the wall at the pub in especially unique costumes. One lady-in-waiting, who appeared in several of the photographs, wore a stunning sapphire and emerald dress trimmed with delicate lace and intricate embroidery.

The next time the woman appeared in the scrapbook, Harriet tapped the photo with her index finger. "I'm almost positive I saw this same picture at the pub. Her outfit is gorgeous."

"That's Heidi Paxton," Andrew said. "She's quite proud of that costume. It's made from vintage fabric—not that it dates back to medieval times, you understand, but it is old. Heidi found it at an estate sale and designed the dress herself."

Will leaned closer to the album. "That is Heidi. I recognize her now."

Harriet's spine tingled. "Heidi Paxton is a reenactor?"

"That's right," Andrew confirmed. "You may have seen her at the festival. She's one of the appraisers."

"I heard that from someone," Harriet said vaguely. How odd that Heidi, who didn't even live in White Church Bay, had a connection with every individual involved in the ghost knight drama.

She'd told Fern that Ivy had argued with Wes. Poppy had seen Wes arguing with Heidi. And she and Andrew were in the same medieval reenactment troupe.

Harriet exchanged a quick glance with Will, who gave her a puzzled expression. If he knew all the clues that she did, he'd understand the tension gripping her shoulders.

"Heidi has been our unofficial director of costumes for a while now," Andrew added, apparently oblivious to Harriet's revelations. "When she joined our troupe, she researched and created new patterns for most of the costumes. Made us all appear more professional. We've even won competitions, thanks to her hard work."

"Did she create the pattern for the knight costume?" Harriet asked.

Andrew grunted. "I suppose now you think Heidi attacked Ivy and Wes."

Harriet's mouth opened, but no words came out. She hadn't intended to offend him, but she was positive that the fabric scrap had come from a costume that was a replica of the one worn by the knight in the painting. Andrew might not be the attacker, but Heidi might be.

"Harriet didn't say that," Will said in a conciliatory tone.

She swallowed to regain her voice. "I was thinking that Heidi might have used the painting at the pub for her inspiration."

"And she'd know who wore costumes like this one." Will held up the print that Harriet had brought with her.

"I suppose she would," Andrew conceded. "But if you talk to her, you don't need to mention that I told you about her."

Since she already felt like she was on thin ice in Andrew's estimation, Harriet didn't ask why.

Apparently Will didn't share Harriet's hesitation. "Any reason why not?"

"She's not one to be underestimated." Andrew abruptly closed the scrapbook and stood. "As soon as I learn the whereabouts of my knight costume, I'll let you know in case you still want to see it. If it's not at home, then it must be at the dry cleaner."

"We'll leave you then," Will said, smiling. He extended his hand as he rose from his seat. "Thank you for showing us your scrapbook. Your wife did a very nice job on it."

Andrew shook Will's hand. "She'll be pleased you think so, Pastor."

Harriet started to gather the dishes, but Andrew stopped her.

"I'll take care of that, Doc…Bailey." He paused and shook his head. "That doesn't sound right when I'm talking to you."

"You can call me Harriet. This is my home now, and I hate to think I've made an enemy with all my questions."

"You haven't. But no man wants his neighbors to believe him capable of violence." He faced Will. "Just because I'm not a church-goer doesn't mean I'd ever do such a thing. I hope you know that."

"I believe you," Will said.

"And I want to apologize for making you uncomfortable," Harriet quickly added. "That wasn't my intent."

She put the print in her bag and followed Andrew to the back door, where they said their goodbyes. Andrew locked the door behind them and pulled down the shade to cover the door-length window.

"I don't think he likes me very much," Harriet said as she and Will trudged up the hill toward the car park.

"His feelings are hurt," Will said. "He'll get over it."

"I wonder what the problem is between him and Heidi. There must be one, if he didn't want us to mention his involvement to her."

"I'd like to know that as well. The special is chicken stew and dumplings over at the Crow's Nest tonight. Would you like to join me for a bite to eat?"

Harriet wanted to say yes, but even without checking the time, she knew she had to decline. At least they'd have time to talk while she drove him to the rectory, but it would have been nice to have a leisurely discussion about what they'd learned—and hadn't learned—from Andrew over a steaming bowl of delicious stew. "I have to get back to the clinic. Nugget is in post-op, remember?"

Will smiled. "I'd forgotten."

They started up the hill again but had only taken a few steps when a flashing neon sign caught Harriet's attention.

"Pizza," she said.

"What?"

"We could take home a pizza." She pointed to the building. "Perhaps Aunt Jinny will stay for some. She'll be interested in what we found out."

"I like this plan." Will's enthusiasm returned. "Let's go."

As they strolled toward the pizza parlor, Harriet called Aunt Jinny to tell her their plan and to see how Nugget was doing. She learned all was well and that her aunt would love a salad.

They placed their order—a large supreme with Caesar salads and garlic knots—then strolled along the cobblestone streets until it was ready. As the sun neared the horizon, they drove past the church so Will could get his car and follow Harriet to Cobble Hill Farm.

While Will and Aunt Jinny set the table and poured beverages, Harriet checked on Nugget. The golden retriever lounged on a large dog bed in front of the living room fireplace instead of staying in a kennel in the clinic. As Aunt Jinny had assured her, Nugget was doing quite well.

According to the memo pad on the mantel, Nugget had eaten a half cup of kibble at six and joined Aunt Jinny and Maxwell on a short walk outside twenty minutes later. Aunt Jinny had written the notations in her singular handwriting which, unlike the popular jokes about doctors and their unreadable scrawls, was amazingly legible.

Harriet checked the retriever's abdominal stitches while talking softly to her. "I'll give you something for the pain in another hour," she murmured. "And maybe a mild sedative so you sleep comfortably through the night. How does that sound?"

Nugget raised a paw in the air, and Harriet grasped it. "We've got a deal."

While enjoying their salads and pizza, Harriet and Will took turns telling Aunt Jinny about their visit with Andrew, his lack of an alibi for the time of Wes's attack, and the missing costume.

"Do you think he's deliberately hiding it?" Aunt Jinny asked. "If the costume was torn, he wouldn't want you to see it." She suddenly paused, fork poised in midair, eyes rounded. "Does he know about the tear?"

"We didn't tell him," Harriet assured her. "I suppose he could have been lying, but I didn't get the sense that he was."

"Neither did I," Will said. "At least, not about that."

"You think he lied about something else?" Aunt Jinny asked.

"I don't like saying he might have," Will hedged. "But I do wonder why he said what he did about Heidi. Almost as if he were pointing us toward her without pointing us toward her, if you know what I mean."

They reviewed the conversation but couldn't come to a consensus on whether Andrew was purposely trying to deflect attention away from himself and onto someone else or not. Neither did they agree on their next step. Harriet wanted to talk to Heidi, but neither Aunt Jinny nor Will could get away during the day, and they didn't like the idea of Harriet talking to the appraiser on her own. Harriet assured them any meeting would take place in public, but they still urged her to wait until one of them could go with her.

She thought they were being overprotective, though they made a fair point. If Heidi had attacked Ivy and Wes, then it was possible she could be dangerous if she felt threatened by Harriet.

After Will and Aunt Jinny left, Harriet finished tidying up the kitchen and made her nighttime rounds to ensure that Maxwell and Nugget were all settled in their respective places for the night. Charlie fended for herself and usually ended up in Harriet's bed.

Sometime tomorrow, despite Aunt Jinny's and Will's warnings, she had to talk to Heidi. It shouldn't be that hard to steer the conversation in such a way to find out where Heidi was when the attacks had taken place. If Heidi had alibis, then Harriet could cross her name off her short list of suspects. If she didn't, then Harriet would tell Van everything she'd learned. That was, if she could get Ivy's permission to tell him about the anonymous note.

One thing at a time.

What could go wrong?

CHAPTER THIRTEEN

Harriet clutched her oversize tote to her side as she approached the pavilion the following afternoon. Naturally, Ivy held court at the entrance.

Harriet greeted her with a warm smile. "The grounds feel so empty now that the carnival is gone."

The company that provided the rides, games, and out-of-town food vendors had packed up and headed for their next destination.

"Thankfully, that part of the Antique Festival has come to an end." Ivy wasn't wearing a hat or a bandage today, though her hair was carefully styled to hide her wound. "Now we can focus on the reason we established this event in the first place."

"Do you hate the carnival that much?"

Ivy averted her gaze. "I suppose not. The rides bring in the families. They might not come if we were strictly showcasing appraisals."

Harriet squeezed Ivy's hand. "It takes a big person to admit something like that. No wonder everyone regards you so highly."

Ivy arched an eyebrow. "Everyone? Then why was I attacked?"

"I wish I could figure that out. However, Will and I were talking to Andrew Ellsworth yesterday. He thinks the world of you."

"Dear Andrew." Ivy's eyes softened as she said his name. "Such a sweet boy. Sadly, he didn't have an easy time as a child. I'm proud of the man he's become." Suddenly her eyes narrowed as she glared at Harriet. "You don't think Andrew attacked me, do you?"

"No. He was at his store at the time," Harriet said, feeling as if she were being reprimanded.

"And you know that how?"

"I talked to him. I found out he's a knight in a medieval reenactment troupe." The words tumbled out as Harriet rushed to explain why she'd thought of Andrew as a suspect. "His costume is almost an exact replica of—"

"I know all about his troupe, and I won't hear another word against him. You, however, need to hear a few words *for* him. He calls me at least once a week to chat. He buys me flowers for Mother's Day, even though there's not much of an age difference between us, and he never forgets my birthday or Christmas. He is not the ghost knight."

"I don't suppose he is." But even as she said it, a possible scenario played out in Harriet's imagination. Andrew could be in cahoots with someone who wore his costume while attacking Ivy, and then Andrew wore it to attack Wes. That would mean he knew about the patch she'd found in Jiffy's mouth, and he wouldn't want it to be identified as coming from his tunic. What if he had lied about his costume being left at the cleaners?

"Your mind is whirling," Ivy said in a warning tone. "I can see it in your eyes."

"I'm just thinking," Harriet said, unwilling to admit she hadn't completely eliminated Andrew as a ghost knight.

"Why are you here, Harriet?" Ivy's question interrupted her thoughts. "Did you decide to take your umbrella stand home?"

"I'm here because I think you should tell Van about the note."

"I won't do that. And I'd appreciate it if you didn't speak of this again. Not to me or anyone else."

When Harriet didn't respond—too many confused thoughts were zinging through her mind—a warm smile lifted Ivy's rouged cheeks. "I know you mean well. But DC Worthington is the one tasked to investigate these awful attacks. Not you."

Her words were similar to Aunt Jinny's. Maybe God was trying to tell her something. Was she stubbornly refusing to listen to His voice? Perhaps she owed Ivy an apology.

"I never meant to upset you," Harriet said. "I know we met a week ago, but with all that's happened, I consider you a friend. I hope you think of me as a friend too."

Ivy smiled. "We *are* friends, Harriet. I adored your grandmother, and your aunt was like an older sister to me in our younger years." Ivy seemed lost for a moment, as if her mind was a million miles away, perhaps revisiting long-ago memories.

"How have you been feeling?" Harriet asked. "Any headaches or nausea?"

"Do you think I'd be here if I wasn't feeling one hundred percent myself?" Ivy asked sharply.

"As a matter of fact, I think you'd be here if you were at ten percent. Thankfully, Aunt Jinny stopped you."

Ivy's smile broadened. "You are a smart one, aren't you? I'm fine. And I'm much better off here than sitting at home and wondering what I'm missing."

"I understand that." Harriet glanced toward the pavilion's entrance. She didn't want to be rude, but she hadn't intended on getting into a lengthy conversation with Ivy. Not when she was here on a mission.

She opened one of the brochures on the counter and looked over the schedule. "I have a gap in appointments right now, so I came to see the appraisals. Have they finished the porcelain figurines yet?"

"No, but they should soon."

"Grandad has an interesting one in his study. A colorful peacock. I almost brought it instead of the umbrella stand."

"Perhaps you should have. Though I still don't understand why that umbrella stand didn't attract more attention. I think it's exquisite. Now, Jinny's gargoyle." Ivy raised her eyes to the heavens as if seeking divine understanding. "I can't imagine anyone taking an interest in that."

Harriet chuckled. "I don't think she cares. She's crazy about Winston."

"Of all the antiques she has in that lovely home of hers, I don't understand why she brought that wretched gargoyle."

Harriet didn't know how to answer that. For the most part, Aunt Jinny was a practical woman, but that made her moments of impracticality and whimsy even more entertaining.

"Speaking of porcelain figurines," Ivy went on. "She must have at least a dozen fine pieces."

Instead of replying, Harriet slid her eyes toward the pavilion. "Would it be okay if I go in?"

"Go ahead. But quietly, in case they're filming a sequence."

Harriet put a finger to her lips. "I promise."

Ivy waved her away.

Once inside, Harriet paused to get her bearings. After all, she wasn't as interested in the items being appraised as she was in the appraiser doing the appraising.

Heidi Paxton.

Pedestals for smaller objects, easels for canvases, and a platform for large items such as furniture were arranged at one end of the large room. A camera crew filmed two women standing beside a porcelain ballerina displayed on a well-lit pedestal. Both smiled as they chatted.

Harriet joined the few onlookers who stood on either side of a rope line and studied the younger of the two women. Her brunette hair was styled in a modern bob instead of being tucked beneath an elaborately coiffed wig, and she wore a fitted sweater dress instead of a medieval-inspired ball gown. Even so, Harriet recognized Heidi from the photograph she'd seen in Andrew's scrapbook.

Though the ballerina was worth less than two hundred pounds, the owner was thrilled that it had been chosen for a televised segment. Heidi's engaging personality and conversational style encouraged the owner—a spry woman who joyfully announced her age as seventy-six—to share her story of how she'd found the figurine in remarkably pristine condition behind a built-in shelf that was being demolished as part of a remodeling project.

When the segment ended, Heidi talked with the woman for a few more moments, impressing Harriet with her personable attitude. The other onlookers followed the camera crew to another display pedestal where another figurine waited to be filmed, but Harriet lingered near Heidi.

Once the women's conversation ended, Harriet approached Heidi with a warm smile. "Ms. Paxton? Hello, I'm Harriet Bailey."

"The veterinarian?" Heidi said. "I've heard about you. Skippy Stiles sang your praises when I saw him over the weekend. He's very grateful for the way you cared for Jiffy. That border collie means the world to him."

"He's a great dog. It's awful that someone hurt him."

"And what about Ivy Chapman?" Heidi asked. "We've all been so concerned about her, but she insists she's okay."

"I spoke to her before I came in. She seems to be fine, though I'm not sure she'd admit it if she wasn't." Harriet gestured toward the camera crew. "Am I keeping you from filming?"

"They'll let me know when they want me." Heidi returned her attention to Harriet. "I heard you inherited Cobble Hill Farm. Did you bring something from your grandfather's estate to be appraised?"

"An umbrella stand that turned out to be a reproduction. But last night I was browsing the Antique Festival website and saw you were appraising porcelain pieces. My grandfather had a small collection, so I brought my favorite." Harriet lifted her bag. "I hoped I could make an appointment to have you look at it while you're in town."

Heidi appeared intrigued. "I have some free time after we film this next segment. It won't take too long. Can you stick around until I'm finished?"

"As long as there aren't any vet emergencies."

Heidi gestured toward a nearby hallway. "A couple of the conference rooms along that corridor have been set aside for the appraisers and production team. We'll go there once I'm done."

"Thank you, that'd be wonderful."

"My pleasure. I'm eager to see what you have."

"Heidi?" someone called.

"That's my cue."

Harriet joined the onlookers again. Shortly after the segment was taped, she and Heidi walked together to a long conference room furnished with a conversational area at one end and a table and chairs at the other. A side table held a variety of snacks and beverages.

Heidi grabbed two bottles of water and offered one to Harriet. Once they were seated in the upholstered club chairs, Harriet pulled a wooden case from her tote bag. She opened the lid and was about to draw the porcelain peacock from its padded case when a knock sounded on the doorframe.

Ivy entered the room, followed by Van. He stared at Harriet, a puzzled expression on his face. "What are you doing here?"

"Heidi is appraising one of Grandad's porcelain statues for me." At Ivy's frown, Harriet's cheeks burned. "Were you looking for me?" Harriet asked Van.

"He's looking for Heidi." Ivy faced the appraiser. "This is Detective Constable Van Worthington. He asked me to introduce you."

"What can I do for you, DC Worthington?" Heidi replied with a slight tremor in her voice. She folded her hands in her lap.

Van pulled a folded sheet of paper from his pocket. "I'm here on official business. Perhaps you'd like to discuss this in private."

Heidi hesitated. Then she lifted her chin, and her expression hardened. "I'm among friends. I have no wish for them to leave, nor any idea of what your 'official business' could possibly be."

"Very well." He stepped into the room and handed her the paper. "This is a warrant giving me the authority to search your lodgings and any possessions you have here at the festival."

Heidi's face paled. "Why would you want to do that?"

"It's explained in the warrant." Van appeared uncomfortable, and Harriet wondered how often his duties required him to perform such a search. Though she was even more curious why the search was necessary. What did he expect to find?

Then, in a flash, she knew. *The costume.* She stared at Van. How did he know about Heidi's connection to the medieval troupe? Perhaps Andrew had told him.

As if Van sensed her reaction, his gaze met hers, and his cheeks reddened.

Heidi raised her head from scanning the warrant, disbelief on her face. "I don't understand. What are you hoping to find?"

Instead of answering her question, Van gestured toward the storage totes, suitcases, and boxes lined up against the far wall. "Do any of those belong to you?"

Heidi pointed to two rectangular plastic bins stacked on top of each other. "Those are mine."

"Thank you." Van set the first bin on the table and removed the lid. It held notebooks, reference guides, and assorted other paraphernalia.

Heidi sat at the table, arms crossed, and glared daggers in Van's direction.

"Do you mind telling me where you were last Tuesday?" he asked her.

"You mean the first day of the festival? I was...around."

"Could you be more specific?" Van asked, keeping his tone polite and respectful.

"I checked in at the White Hart inn, I walked around the village, and I came here to get a peek at what people were bringing in for the appraisers."

"Can anyone vouch for that?"

"I saw a few people I know. Ivy, for instance."

Ivy joined her at the table. "We did visit for a few minutes."

"Before you went to the cave?"

"Obviously," she said, sounding annoyed. "Considering that after I went to the cave, I went to the hospital."

Harriet pressed her lips together to keep from asking the questions bombarding her brain. Van wouldn't appreciate her interruption, and she didn't want to give him an excuse to send her away. But the questions were there—*Was that before or after Ivy's argument with Wes? What did Ivy and Heidi talk about? Did Heidi try to comfort Ivy, or was she curious as to the argument? Or did they also argue? And what about the argument between Heidi and Wes that Poppy said she witnessed?*

Though that argument had taken place after the helicopter rescue, the two arguments could be related. Ivy might have told Heidi about her quarrel with Wes and then perhaps Heidi confronted him. If only Harriet understood the connection between these three people, which must go beyond their expertise and appreciation of antiques.

"What did you talk about?" Van asked, his gaze taking in both Ivy and Heidi. Harriet inwardly applauded the DC.

"Nothing in particular," Ivy said, her tone evasive. "Just a bit of a catch-up."

"Now, Ivy," Heidi said. "It was a little more than that. You'll forgive me, I hope, but I think the detective constable should know that you and Wes had words." She eyed Van. "Unless you already know about their argument."

"Can't say that I do." He watched Ivy in expectant silence.

Ivy glared at Heidi then smiled sweetly at Van. "A personal disagreement. That's all."

"Both you and Mr. Brinley were attacked by this ghost knight," Van said. "And I'm just now finding out that you argued with each other before the attacks happened? That argument could be an important clue to the attacker's identity."

"I don't see how," Ivy replied. "But if you must know, I'll tell you. Wes promised to bring a certain sculpture to be appraised. When I asked him about it, he said Emma had already given it to me. But she hadn't, and then Wes had the nerve to accuse me of losing it." Her voice rose as she grew angrier recalling the incident. "That's absolute nonsense, of course."

"Where is this sculpture now?" Van asked.

"Ask Wes," Ivy retorted. "I certainly haven't seen it."

Van glanced at Harriet. "Do you think this sculpture has anything to do with the attacks?"

Surprised that he'd asked her that question, Harriet fumbled over her answer. "I wish I knew. It seems to have disappeared though. When we talked at the carnival, Wes told me he didn't know where it was."

"Meaning you knew about this argument too."

Harriet's cheeks burned as Van started to put the items back in the bin.

"I'll do that," Heidi said, stopping him. "Everything must be packed in a certain way for it to fit."

Van left her to it and placed the second bin on the table next to the first. He set the lid on the floor then removed a shoebox of assorted office supplies—scissors, paper clips, pens, sticky notes, tape, and a stapler—then another with monogrammed notecards.

From her vantage point, Harriet couldn't see into the box, but when Van reached in again and riffled through the contents, he suddenly frowned. Then he pulled a scarlet tunic embroidered with gold thread from beneath the other items.

"What's this?" he asked.

Heidi's eyes widened, and she inhaled sharply. "How did that get in there?"

"You tell me." Van held the tunic by the shoulders and gently spread it out on the table. "Don't touch it," he warned as Harriet reached to straighten a sleeve.

"It's torn," she said, her fingers itching to smooth out the fabric. She bent closer and scrutinized a dark stain on the front of the tunic. "Is that…?"

"The lab will have to tell us." Van stepped toward Heidi with clear reluctance. "I'm sorry, Ms. Paxton. You're under arrest on suspicion of assault upon Ivy Chapman and Wes Brinley." He proceeded to recite the police caution.

"But I didn't attack them," Heidi protested. "I don't know how that tunic got in my bin. It's not mine, and I certainly didn't put it there."

"Do you know who it belongs to?" Harriet asked. "I've been told that you design these costumes for the medieval reenactors."

Heidi stared at her in surprise and then swept her gaze over the tunic.

"Is that true?" Van asked, obviously caught off guard. "Did you make this?"

"I'm not a seamstress," Heidi said irritably. "I designed it. The basic costume for the knights is similar, but the embroidery patterns vary. I don't keep track of which patterns the reenactors choose for their outfits."

"It may belong to Andrew Ellsworth," Harriet said quietly.

"I already told you that Andrew isn't the ghost knight," Ivy said sharply. "He wouldn't do such a thing."

"I'm only sharing what I know," Harriet said and stared pointedly at Ivy. "Maybe we all should do that."

Ivy harrumphed and turned her head. Apparently, she still didn't intend to tell Van about the note that lured her to the cave. Or tell anyone who she thought had written it. Even though Harriet now knew that Fern had written the note, that didn't change the fact that Ivy had a secret. And what if that "secret" had attacked her and Wes?

Harriet's thoughts returned to an earlier supposition. What if Andrew had attacked Wes and someone else had attacked Ivy? Van could be wrong in his assumption that the same person had attacked them both.

Harriet's gaze shifted to Heidi. Were she and Andrew in on the attacks together? Harriet mentally shook her head. Andrew and Heidi? A devoted friend of Ivy's teaming up with a woman he claimed not to trust? That didn't make any sense.

And yet, Heidi had Andrew's tunic. That tunic, stained with blood, was missing a triangular scrap of fabric with an identical embroidery pattern as the scrap found in Jiffy's mouth.

Harriet couldn't believe that more evidence had led to more questions—and no answers.

CHAPTER FOURTEEN

Harriet parked the Beast back at the clinic. She debated whether to go first to the kitchen to put the teakettle on or to check in with Polly. After the shock of Heidi's arrest, Harriet could use a few more minutes to herself. Especially as she relived the moment Van placed handcuffs on Heidi's wrists then escorted her from the room. Before she went through the doorway, Heidi had looked straight at Harriet, her eyes frightened and pleading.

But pleading for what?

Nothing Harriet could do would stop Van from arresting Heidi. Not when the scarlet tunic that must have been worn by the ghost knight had been found in her possession.

Yet Heidi had appeared genuinely shocked when Van had taken the tunic from her bin. Even more shocked than Andrew had been when he realized Harriet suspected him. And Harriet was certain that neither had been acting.

Her mental debate ended when a familiar vehicle parked in front of the clinic door. Her pulse quickened at this unforeseen opportunity to confirm Andrew's story that he had been at his shop when Ivy had been attacked.

Miss Jane Birtwhistle hadn't been on the afternoon schedule when Harriet checked it before going to the pavilion. Either one of her feline friends needed emergency care, or another stray had appeared at her cottage door. If the latter, then that stray would need to be checked for parasites and given vaccinations so it could officially join the Birtwhistle clowder, or group of cats. How many would that make? Perhaps a baker's dozen or more.

Harriet slid from her vehicle and greeted Jane as she emerged with a cat carrier in one hand and a round tin, no doubt filled with home-baked goodies, in the other.

"I called Polly," Jane said, "and she said I could come in. But if you're leaving, I can come back another time."

"I'm arriving, so your timing is fine," Harriet said as she took the carrier and peered through the mesh at the yowling kitten inside. "What are you so upset about, little one?"

"She's a noisy one, all right. Though can you blame the tyke? I took a ramble along the shore and found her huddled among the rocks as the waves swept over her."

"How awful." Harriet didn't even want to imagine how such a young kitten had ended up someplace like that.

"If she hadn't been so loud, I would never have heard her." Jane's pale blue eyes glistened, and she patted the carrier as if to reassure its unhappy occupant that all would be well. "All wet and covered with sand, she was. But I cleaned her up best I could before bringing her here."

"I'm eager to meet her." Harriet followed Jane into the clinic, waved to Polly, who was on the phone, and led the way to the nearest exam room. "Did she mind being handled?"

"I don't think she's used to it. My coat sleeves and gloves saved me from her scratches. I tucked her in my hat, and the poor little thing was so worn out from fear and crying that she was sound asleep within minutes."

Harriet set the carrier on the exam table. "We'll give her a chance to come out of the carrier on her own, but first I'll get a towel in case we need it."

Harriet gathered the necessary supplies then opened the carrier door. The kitten, silent now, stretched her head out far enough to scan the room for any sign of danger with her large amber eyes. Her sleek black fur faded to gray above those curious eyes, giving her the appearance of having light-colored eyebrows.

She meowed at Jane, who stood across the table from Harriet, then padded toward her, her thin tail held high. She sniffed Jane's fingers then playfully tapped them with her paw.

Harriet chuckled. "You have a new friend."

"She forgives me even though I was the big meanie who gave her a bath." Jane gazed lovingly at the tiny sprite then smiled at Harriet. "About seven to eight weeks, would you say?"

"I believe so." Harriet smiled. She had recognized the depth of Jane's feline experience soon after she arrived in Yorkshire.

"I checked around for the mother and any other kittens, but they were nowhere to be found."

"At least you found this one." Harriet was suddenly reminded of the old story about a beach covered in starfish. A young boy took as many as he could to the shallow waves. When someone told him he was wasting his time because he couldn't save them all, he held out the ones in his hands. "But I can save these," he said. Not even Jane, with her loving heart and generous spirit, could save all the lost cats in Yorkshire. But that didn't stop her from trying.

"Did you give her a name?"

"I was thinking Pippin," Jane replied as the kitten snuggled against her.

"It suits her." Amazingly, now that Pippin was out of the carrier, she didn't mind being handled. Instead of yowling, she purred contentedly while Harriet weighed her and examined her teeth. "You're right about her age. She's small though."

"She always will be," Jane said, smiling at Harriet. "But not for lack of food or good care. I'll always be grateful for how kind you were to Mittens when he couldn't take those awful pills. You reminded me of your grandfather."

The compliment warmed Harriet's heart. Mittens, a handsome tuxedo cat with hyperthyroidism, had been with Jane for twelve years. Of her dozen or so cats, he was the favorite. Since he couldn't take the pills, Harriet had prescribed an ear paste, which had worked wonders.

"You're very kind. I'm glad Mittens is doing so well."

"Me too."

Harriet prepared the kitten's vaccines. Now was the time to ask about Andrew, but how could she broach the subject without being obvious?

"I saw Ivy Chapman at the pavilion a little while ago. She seems to be doing much better after her ordeal at the cave."

"Such an awful thing that was," Jane replied in a sympathetic tone. "Everyone was talking about it."

"The news did get around quickly. That's one thing I love about this place. People truly watch out for one another."

"I was shopping for a birthday gift when I heard the news. We were all so shocked. Why, I thought Andrew might faint or something."

So Andrew had told the truth. He'd been with Jane, so he couldn't have been the one who attacked Ivy. But that didn't mean he hadn't attacked Wes. And yet the costume found in Heidi's bin had likely been worn by the ghost knight who attacked Ivy and Jiffy. Which meant either Heidi was the ghost knight, or someone had hidden the tunic in her bin.

Because no one would find it there? Or was it a deliberate attempt to frame the appraiser?

Later that afternoon, Harriet tidied up the clinic, made sure the examination rooms were stocked for the next day, and then wandered to the reception area. Polly stood by the door, staring at her watch. Harriet glanced at the wall clock. The little hand was on the four, and the big hand was a dog's hair away from the twelve while the second hand made its upward sweep. Less than twenty seconds until four o'clock. Polly reached for the Open sign.

"Eager to leave?" Harriet asked, amusement in her voice. "Big plans this evening?"

Polly shot her an annoyed look as she flipped the sign and locked the door. "No and no," she said as she returned to her desk to close her computer. "It's time you and I had a talk."

A talk? Harriet's amusement faded to concern. "Is something wrong?"

"As a matter of fact, yes." Polly handed a brochure to Harriet then crossed her arms. "What do you know about this?"

Puzzled, Harriet scanned the brochure's cover, which showed a whale surfacing in front of a sightseeing boat. "The whale-watching expedition. Did Van give you this?"

"He stopped by here shortly after you left for the pavilion." Polly plopped into a nearby chair. "He has VIP tickets."

"He told me." Harriet sat next to her. "What did you say when he asked you?"

"At first, I was too surprised to say anything." Polly massaged her temples. "And then he said he hoped I'd agree to go even if I didn't want to go, which didn't make any sense."

Harriet frantically tried to recall, word for word, the conversation she'd had with Van. That didn't quite sound like the advice she'd given him. But she could barely remember the discussion. Her thoughts since then had been too consumed with her hunt for the ghost knight to think of much else.

Polly went on. "Then I said—because I didn't know what else to say—that I hadn't been on one of those excursions in a couple of years. And then he said that you didn't know if I liked whale-watching."

"I don't think I said *that*," Harriet protested.

Polly straightened then shifted sideways in her seat to face Harriet. "You knew he was going to ask me?"

"I wasn't sure. In fact, I'm not sure he was sure at the time." Harriet offered an apologetic smile. "I'm sorry I didn't warn you, but I didn't think it was my place to do so."

"Oh, please." Polly dismissed the apology with a wave of her hand. "I'm not mad. I don't know what I am."

Harriet widened her eyes. "You mean you said yes?"

"I didn't have a chance to say yes or no," Polly declared, throwing her arms wide in a dramatic gesture. "Van got a phone call, and it must have been serious, because he left in a rush with barely a goodbye." She deflated, and her voice was barely above a whisper. "I thought he'd call, but so far nothing. Not even a text."

Harriet hardly knew what to think. Polly seemed genuinely disappointed that Van hadn't contacted her. But she'd never shown much interest in him before. As far as Harriet knew, they'd only gone out a couple of times, and Polly had made it very clear that those were friendly get-togethers, not romantic ones.

"I'm sure he'll be in touch," she said, trying to reassure Polly while questioning whether Polly needed—or even wanted—reassurance. "I imagine that call was about Heidi Paxton, one of the festival appraisers. She's been arrested as a likely suspect in the attack on Ivy."

"I know her. Not very well, but she's one of the regulars that Ivy invites back year after year."

As Polly spoke, Harriet suddenly recalled Van's surprise that she was with Heidi when he arrived with the search warrant. "You didn't tell Van I was at the pavilion, did you? He seemed surprised to find me there."

"When I told him you were out, he asked if you were on a farm call, or hunting for the ghost knight," Polly replied. "I wasn't sure whether he was joking. So I said you definitely weren't on a farm call. Then the clinic phone rang, so we couldn't get into it any deeper. As soon as I hung up, he gave me the brochure and told me about the tickets."

No wonder Van had been surprised to see her at the pavilion. If he thought Harriet was investigating the ghost knight, which was true, then he'd want to know why she was with Heidi. And why she was talking to Heidi without informing him. Hopefully, he'd understand that she couldn't tell him about her suspicions of Heidi's involvement without proof.

"Did Van actually arrest Heidi at the pavilion?" Polly asked. "In front of everybody?"

"No one was there but Ivy and me." But no doubt the news was already the topic of whispered gossip among the locals in the village. Polly might as well hear the details from a firsthand witness. And maybe talking over the event would help Harriet untangle her thoughts about it.

In a few months, Polly had become not only the clinic receptionist but also a good friend. She'd also been Harriet's mystery-solving sidekick as they'd investigated other crimes and strange happenings. Due to the circumstances, Harriet had instead confided in Aunt Jinny and Will for this mystery. Perhaps it was past time to share everything she knew with Polly—except for Ivy's note, of course—and get her perspective.

"Would you like a cup of tea?"

"I'd love one." Polly rose and smoothed the wrinkles out of her pants. The orange streak in her hair had been replaced by a deep gold that complemented her chunky necklace and earrings. "You go ahead, and I'll close up."

Harriet headed for the kitchen, followed by Maxwell and Charlie. Both animals trotted to the cabinet where Harriet kept their treats. She melted at the pleading in their eyes, both the dachshund's deep brown ones and the calico's yellow ones.

"One apiece," she told them, and was rewarded with a joyful bark from Maxwell and a long meow from Charlie. She gave them their treats and a pat then filled the kettle.

By the time Polly arrived, the table was set with ceramic mugs, the caddy of assorted tea bags, a small oval tray holding sugar, honey, and lemon wedges, and the snack tin. When the kettle whistled, Harriet poured the boiling water into their mugs.

"I had hoped Ivy's attacker would turn out to be someone we didn't know," Polly said as she took her seat. "Why would Heidi do something so awful?"

The image of Heidi, hands cuffed, pausing in the doorway to stare over her shoulder at Harriet with such desperation in her eyes, hit Harriet again. The moment haunted her.

"I'm not sure she did."

"Then why did Van arrest her?" Polly sounded almost defensive, as if Harriet had accused the DC of wrongdoing.

Harriet pushed that thought aside. "He found the ghost knight's tunic in one of her bins. It was stained with blood, and a small part of the sleeve was missing."

"A triangular piece?" Polly had apparently read Jiffy's veterinary record before filing it, so she knew about the scrap of fabric.

"Like the one I found in Jiffy's mouth."

Polly stirred sugar into her tea. "Then why don't you think she's guilty? Does she have an alibi?"

Harriet selected a shortbread biscuit from the tin and broke it in half to dunk into her tea. "We've had so little time to talk, what with the festival and my being away from the clinic more often than usual. Here's what I know."

Polly listened intently, asking questions here and there, as Harriet told her about Fern's claim that Heidi had seen Ivy arguing with Wes before her attack in the cave and Poppy Schofield's claim that she had seen Heidi arguing with Wes after the helicopter rescued Ivy and Jiffy. They also talked about the legend of the lost drummer boy, Harriet and Will's trip to Richmond, and their talk with Andrew Ellsworth. How Andrew had said his knight costume was at the dry cleaner and Jane Birtwhistle's confirmation of his alibi.

Keeping her word to Van, she didn't mention the mysterious 999 call that Wes couldn't have made. She also kept Ivy's note to herself.

"That was Andrew's costume in Heidi's bin?" Polly asked.

"Or one exactly like it."

"But you think Heidi is innocent."

"She didn't know the tunic was in the bin, that's for sure. She was as shocked by it as I was. But what if she and Andrew are partners?"

"You mean there are two ghost knights?"

"There could be. What if Heidi wore the costume and attacked Ivy, and then Andrew wore it and attacked Wes?" Harriet reached for another shortbread biscuit.

"Say you're right that Heidi and Andrew were partners in this," Polly said. "Does that mean Andrew put the costume in Heidi's bin? Why would he try to frame her when she could incriminate him too?"

As they finished their tea, the two friends talked over the mystery of the ghost knight, offering up ever more improbable theories until they were crying with laughter at how far-fetched their what-ifs had become.

"We shouldn't make fun," Polly said as she carried her mug to the sink. "But at the core, the entire thing is so ludicrous. Why did the attacker dress up in the first place? It all seems unnecessarily theatrical."

"I hadn't thought of it that way," Harriet replied, "but you're right."

Unfortunately, Polly's insight didn't shed any light on solving the mystery.

Together they put away the tea things and tidied the kitchen. Polly's phone chirped, and she checked the screen. Her frown indicated that whoever had sent the text wasn't the person she hoped to hear from.

"It's Mum," she said as she tapped out her response.

"Would you like me to drive you home?" Harriet offered. "It's no trouble."

Polly glanced out the window at the clear blue sky. "There's plenty of time to make it home before sunset. I'll be perfectly safe. And if a ghost knight comes for me, he'll be sorry." She gave Harriet a fierce scowl.

Harriet chuckled, and they walked to the barn where Polly had stored her bike in case it rained.

"I'm sure he'll call," Harriet said as Polly strapped on her helmet.

"Who?" Polly's innocent expression didn't fool Harriet.

Harriet didn't even try to explain what she'd told Van—that a woman might say yes to a man she wanted to go out with no matter what he'd planned for the date. But that must have been what he was referring to when he told Polly he hoped she'd say yes even if she didn't like such excursions.

Considering Polly's disappointed frown and her behavior earlier, Harriet hoped Van called her soon. She didn't need detective skills to intuit Polly planned to say yes. Though whether it was because she wanted to see the whales or be with Van, Harriet couldn't be sure.

Harriet gave a final wave as Polly pedaled toward the main road, then her phone rang as she started back to the house. *Unknown Caller* appeared on the screen, but that wasn't unusual. Mentally preparing herself for an emergency call, she answered.

"This is Heidi Paxton," the shaky voice said. "I need to talk to you. It's important."

CHAPTER FIFTEEN

Once again, Will waited outside the rectory when Harriet parked in front of the entrance. She'd agreed to Heidi's insistent request on the condition that someone else came with her. Harriet had intended to ask Aunt Jinny, but to her surprise, Heidi suggested that the pastor of White Church join them.

Will slid into the passenger seat of the Beast and fastened his seat belt. On the short drive to the car park and the walk to the Crow's Nest, Harriet brought him up to date on everything that had happened that afternoon. Will listened as Harriet began with her ruse of taking the porcelain peacock for Heidi to appraise so she could talk to her and ended with Heidi's desperate phone call asking Harriet to meet her.

"What about the peacock?" Will teased. "Is it worth more than the umbrella stand?"

"No idea," Harriet said, appreciating how he lightened the mood. "She didn't even see it."

They entered the pub. The Crow's Nest was a favorite among the locals and served mouthwatering comfort food. They spotted Heidi at a rear table and took seats across from her. A brown stocking cap covered her brunette hair, and dark glasses hid her eyes.

"Thank you for coming." Her voice sounded steadier than during her phone call, but her pale face and tense shoulders betrayed her anxiety. "I ordered an appetizer sampler. My treat." A wavery smile revealed tiny lines around her mouth.

"We're glad to be here," Will said warmly. Harriet darted a thankful glance his way. She had no idea what to say to Heidi. "Though I'm also surprised. My understanding is that you were arrested a few hours ago."

Heidi removed the glasses. Even in the pub's dim lighting, Harriet noted her puffy eyes.

"I found a very good attorney who pointed out that the evidence is circumstantial," she said. "The conference room was unlocked and unguarded. Anyone could have planted that tunic among my belongings. And someone *did* plant it. My fingerprints won't be found on it, because I never touched it." Her gaze held Harriet's. "And I didn't attack anyone."

A waiter arrived with glasses, plates, a pitcher of soda, and a platter of stuffed mushrooms, sausage rolls, bacon-wrapped dates, scones, and beef Wellington bites.

"Would you like anything else?" Heidi asked as she poured the soda into their glasses.

"This is more than enough," Harriet said. And overly generous. Was Heidi trying to befriend them? Or bribe them? Neither thought was kind, and Harriet immediately regretted them. And yet how could she not be suspicious? Of all the people Heidi knew in White Church Bay, why had she chosen to call Harriet? Why not Ivy? Or Wes? He'd been released from the hospital, though Harriet didn't know if he'd returned to work or not.

"Everything smells delicious, as usual." Will turned to Harriet and gestured to the dates. "Have you had these before?"

She wasn't sure how he could act so natural when they were sitting across from a woman who'd been arrested mere hours before for assault. But if he could, so could she.

"I haven't, but I'm eager to try one."

"They're sometimes called devils on horseback," he said with a chuckle. "Despite the name, they're one of my favorites. The dates are stuffed with cheese, and the bacon is glazed with maple syrup and a dash of hot sauce."

"Sounds intriguing." Harriet added one to her plate along with her other choices. "Who doesn't love bacon and maple syrup?"

Heidi used her knife and fork to cut a bite from her sausage roll. "I know you're wondering why I called you."

"Considering we only met today, yes I am," Harriet admitted.

"We formally met today," Heidi replied. "But I know a great deal about you. Anyone who spent much time with Old Doc Bailey has heard all about his American granddaughter."

"You knew my grandfather?"

"I've been at the Antique Festival almost every year since I graduated university." Heidi blinked back sudden tears. "I am very sorry for your loss. Harold was a kind and generous man."

The lump in Harriet's throat kept her from replying. She sipped her soda instead.

"I don't have an alibi for Ivy's attack," Heidi continued. "That's because I took a very long ramble and ended up at Cobble Hill Farm."

Harriet was puzzled. "You went to the clinic?"

"To the art gallery," Heidi said. "Whenever I'm in the area, I try to stop in. There's something uplifting and restful about Harold's paintings. Almost like a tonic."

Will smiled. "That's true. I have one of his paintings in the rectory. He certainly had a gift."

"This is the first time I've been in White Church Bay since his passing." Heidi talked faster, as if she couldn't get the words out fast enough. "When I saw where I was, I thought to go in. To pay my respects, you see. But too many other people were there, so I changed my mind. I didn't want an audience for my grief." Her voice caught.

Harriet exchanged a glance with Will. The sympathy in his eyes about did her in, but then one side of his mouth lifted in a tiny, gentle smile, as if he understood the turmoil going on inside her.

Part of her wanted to ask Heidi if anyone saw her there. After all, the woman couldn't prove she'd been anywhere near the gallery. But her heart was also affected by Heidi's appreciation of Grandad's art.

"Your grandfather touched many lives with his love for people and their animals," Will told Harriet. "Not to mention his talent for capturing that special personal spark. And, perhaps most of all, he touched them with his compassion."

"He was a wonderful man." Harriet took a deep breath and faced Heidi. "How well do you know Wes Brinley? The two of you were seen arguing after the medical helicopter left the festival grounds."

Will helped himself to another scone. "Do you have an alibi for the time Wes was attacked?"

Heidi's cheeks reddened. "That's why I asked you to come, Pastor. Being arrested and handcuffed"—she shuddered—"I never want to go through something like that again."

Will spoke in a kind tone. "Why would you?"

"Because sometimes I cheat people. Though only those who can afford the loss." Tears shimmered in her eyes, and she brushed them away. "You're right," she said to Harriet. "I saw Wes arguing with Ivy before she disappeared. I thought he was telling Ivy about his suspicions of me. I didn't want them to see me, so I hurried away."

"And ended up at the gallery?" Harriet didn't know whether to be angry or hurt. Had everything Heidi had said before been nothing but sentimental drivel?

"What I said was true," Heidi insisted, as if recognizing the disconnect between her two stories. "It was as if something led me there, to a place of refuge. And I felt such a sense of peace when I left, even though I hadn't gone inside the gallery. But when I got back to the festival, there was Wes. He was upset, and we blew up at each other. I accused him of bad-mouthing me to Ivy, and he accused me of cheating one of his customers. In this particular instance, I was innocent, but he wouldn't believe me."

Harriet wasn't quite ready to believe Heidi either, but she pushed her aggrieved feelings aside. Heidi had managed to divert the conversation to ground they'd already covered, and Harriet had had enough. She pushed her plate forward, crossed her arms, and rested them on the table. "Where were you when Wes was attacked?"

Heidi's eyes narrowed slightly at the direct question, but she quickly recovered and gave an almost convincing performance of a distraught woman doing her best not to cry. "I was with a client, Sir Halston Dahlbury. He'll vouch for me."

Will pulled his phone from his pocket. "Do you have his contact info?"

While Heidi texted the info to Will, Harriet nibbled on a stuffed mushroom and went back over the conversation. Heidi had confessed to being a cheat, but what did that mean? Then she'd tossed out a name that sounded made-up. This Dahlbury fellow could be anyone. Maybe someone who would lie for Heidi.

"I'll give Sir Halston a call," Will said, tapping his screen.

Harriet rested her fingers on Will's phone before he connected the call. "Maybe we should visit him instead," she suggested, forcing a smile at Heidi. "After all, anyone could be on the other end of that line."

"Halston isn't a friend," Heidi said. "And our meeting wasn't a cordial one." She focused her attention on Will. "He caught me low-balling an appraisal so I could purchase the item at a discount then resell it for a higher profit. I promised him I'd never do it again, and now I'm telling you."

"Why is that?" Will asked.

"I can't tell the detective constable about Halston without admitting fraud, which I prefer not to do," Heidi replied. "But don't you see? Now you can tell him that I had a alibi for the time of Wes's attack. And then you can tell him that you have clergy privilege, and he'll believe you without ever hearing Halston's name."

Will's face was set in stone, except for the twitch in his jaw and the appalled expression in his eyes. Harriet, though astonished at Heidi's audacity, couldn't stop a sharp laugh from passing her lips.

The awkward noise seemed to snap Will out of his trance. "That's not how a confession works," he said.

Heidi appeared confused. "You're a pastor. You're not allowed to tell the police anything I tell you in confidence."

"I'm not a pastor," Harriet said. "What's to stop me from telling the DC?"

"I would hope your own integrity," Heidi retorted. "This conversation is confidential. When you talk to Halston, please tell him hello from me and give him my thanks for being so understanding. Now I must run." She put on the dark glasses and rose from her seat. "I'm sorry I didn't get to appraise your grandfather's figurine this afternoon. Maybe another time."

"In your dreams," Harriet muttered, but Heidi was already headed toward the exit.

Will gaped at her. "What just happened?"

"I guess she named you her spiritual confessor. Please tell me I'm not bound by any confidentiality dictates."

"You're not." He lifted his phone. "We might as well see what this Halston Dahlbury has to say."

When the call went to voice mail, Will left a message. "This is Pastor Will Knight from White Church. I need to speak to you about a meeting you had with Heidi Paxton a few days ago. Please call me at your earliest convenience."

As he hung up, the waiter arrived. "Will you be having any of our desserts tonight? Our special is an apple and blackberry Charlotte served with hand-dipped vanilla ice cream."

Will arched a questioning eyebrow in Harriet's direction.

"None for me, thanks." Though the appetizers were delicious, Harriet hadn't enjoyed them as much as she might have under different circumstances. Still, they'd been filling.

Will smiled at the waiter. "Maybe another time."

"No problem." The young man placed the check face down on the table. "I'll take that whenever you're ready, sir."

"I think there's been a mistake," Will said. "The other woman who was with us said she would take care of the bill."

The waiter shook his head. "Maybe she forgot."

Harriet didn't believe that, and from Will's expression, he didn't either. She started to pull out her wallet, but he stopped her.

"I've got it."

"At least let me pay half."

"You can pay next time. We'll come back for the apple and blackberry Charlotte."

Once the bill was settled, they left the pub and walked to the car park. The streetlamps spread pools of light over the sidewalk and onto the cobblestone street. A sliver of moon, silvery white against the dark sky, was at times obscured by fast-moving clouds.

"I was ready to believe Heidi's story about going to the art gallery until she walked out without paying the bill," Harriet said. "Now I'm not sure what to think."

"Me either. Not about Heidi anyway. But I've been thinking about your theory that she attacked Ivy and Andrew attacked Wes."

They reached a set of stairs and paused as a trio of teens descended. The boys exchanged greetings with Will and glanced curiously at Harriet.

Will continued the conversation once they were out of earshot. "If Andrew attacked Wes, I think you would have found him passed out on the floor too."

"Why do you say that?" Harriet asked as she and Will climbed the stairs.

"He can't stand the sight of blood. Never could. He doesn't even play on the village cricket team anymore because a few years ago a player on the other team got hit in the nose with the ball. It was barely a trickle, but next thing we knew, Andrew was out cold on the ground."

"If Heidi is telling the truth about being with this Halston Dahlbury and Andrew would have fainted at the sight of Wes's head wound," Harriet said, "then we have no suspects for his attack."

"And yet the ghost knight must be a real person. The costume found in Heidi's bin proves that, along with the victims' injuries and testimonies."

"Someone must have stolen the costume from the dry cleaner."

"If only we knew who."

They reached the top step, and Harriet suddenly stopped. "Poppy Schofield."

Will paused beside her and leaned against the rail. "You think Poppy stole the costume?"

"Not necessarily." Harriet paused and took a deep breath while she gathered her thoughts. "Poppy accused Wes of lying to her about the value of her Austrian porcelain platter. Heidi apparently did the same thing to this Halston Dahlbury. Maybe Heidi and Wes were partners in crime."

Will chuckled. "Is that right?"

"You know what I mean. Maybe I should have another talk with Poppy."

"And maybe I should talk to Wes."

"If he hadn't been attacked," Harriet said, "he'd still be my prime suspect for the attack on Ivy."

"Are we positive his wound wasn't self-inflicted? Emma said the doctor couldn't say for sure."

"The medics didn't think so, and neither did Van. And neither do I. He was too far from the counter."

Will's phone buzzed. "A text from Ivy." His eyes narrowed. "It says, 'Would it be convenient for you to come to my house as soon as possible? Bring Harriet.'"

"That's odd. I wonder what she wants."

"There's one way to find out." Will's thumbs were poised over the phone's screen. "What should I tell her?"

"That we're on our way."

And dying with curiosity. *No, not dying!* Harriet mentally erased that verb from her thought. But definitely curious. What was Ivy up to now?

CHAPTER SIXTEEN

Ivy ushered Harriet and Will into her parlor, where a well-appointed tea trolley stood beside her chair and a rotund man in a brown suit stood by the fireplace. With his hands behind his back and straight posture, dark hair, and penetrating gaze, Harriet's immediate impression was that he'd stepped straight out of the pages of an Agatha Christie novel. He appeared much as Harriet imagined Hercule Poirot, except this man was decidedly British and lacked the fictional detective's famous mustache.

"Allow me to introduce you to a dear friend," Ivy said, giving Harriet a pointed look.

Dear friend? Did Ivy mean this was the man she had believed to be the note writer?

"Dr. Harriet Bailey, Pastor Will Knight," Ivy continued, gesturing to each. "May I present Sir Halston Dahlbury? He is a collector of fine antiques with a shop in Truro."

"All the way from Cornwall?" Will asked as the two men shook hands. "You're about as far from home as you can be and still be in England."

"I try not to miss the Antique Festival," Halston replied. "I always find a treasure or two to take home with me."

"Please sit, and we'll have our tea," Ivy urged. "You must be curious about why I invited you here on such short notice. Halston was here when you called, Will. His phone was silenced, so he missed it."

"I'm sorry about that." Halston settled in the chair on the other side of the table from Ivy as if he belonged there.

Harriet noticed a pair of masculine reading glasses and its case alongside a thin leatherbound book. Had Halston and Ivy been enjoying a quiet evening together before Will called? Was that thin book a volume of romantic poetry?

She sneaked a questioning glance in Ivy's direction before joining Will on the couch. Ivy's cheeks flushed, and she pursed her lips.

"I played your message for Ivy," Halston continued. "She knows everyone in White Church Bay, so I was certain she'd be acquainted with the local pastor. I wished to know more about you before I returned your call. Especially since you mentioned Ms. Paxton."

"I told him you were a respectable and upright young man," Ivy said while pouring the tea. She passed around a caddy of tiny sandwiches and bite-size treats. "I assume Heidi told you of the meeting she had with Halston. We wonder why she would do that."

"She asked Harriet and me to join her at the Crow's Nest," Will started to explain, but Ivy interrupted him with a gasp.

Her eyes grew large and her gaze piercing. "Isn't she in jail?"

"Apparently she has a good lawyer," Harriet replied. "The sole evidence thus far is circumstantial. Anyone could have hidden the tunic in her bin."

"What about an alibi?" Ivy demanded, her tone indignant.

"That's why I called." Will recounted what Heidi had told them—that she was at the art gallery when Ivy was attacked and with Halston when Wes was attacked.

"She's a piece of work, that one," Halston said, sharing a glance with Ivy after Will finished his account.

"I agree," Harriet said. "She even stuck Will with the check after telling us she'd taken care of it."

"I'm not surprised." Ivy set her teacup and saucer on the table and folded her hands in her lap. "After you called, Halston told me how she tried to cheat one of our participants. That's when I invited you both here. Something must be done without causing a scandal for the Antique Festival or for Halston." Ivy lowered her gaze and clutched her hands so hard that her knuckles turned white.

"Now, Ivy," Halston said tenderly, "everything will be all right. Even if the waves crash over us in a rousing storm, the sea will eventually quiet again. You'll see."

"And leave what kind of wreckage in its wake?" Ivy's voice grew shrill. "The festival will survive, but will you?"

Will leaned toward Ivy. "What are you afraid will happen to Halston?"

"She said she'd ruin him if he told anyone what she'd done." The words spilled out in a rush. "That she'd post bad reviews about his shop and get her friends to do the same."

Halston fidgeted with a button on his waistcoat. "I'm ashamed to admit I didn't stand up to her. One reads stories about such things. People's livelihoods being destroyed by social media. I don't much understand it myself, but she seemed so confident in her ability to ruin my reputation."

That was why Heidi hadn't been concerned that Halston would expose her. Then she tried to trick Will into protecting her. If he didn't, would she try to ruin his reputation too?

The conversation continued while they finished their tea. Halston was willing to go to the DC with his story, but Ivy feared the consequences if he did so. It wouldn't do any good for Will to tell Van what Heidi had told him unless Halston also told his side of the story.

Harriet was torn. She had the option of telling Van that Heidi confessed to being a cheat, but were low appraisals against the law? Perhaps what Heidi feared was bad publicity, since she'd threatened the person who had firsthand knowledge of her fraud.

Suddenly, Halston stood. "If good men do nothing, et cetera." He gazed at Ivy. "I want to be a good man."

To Harriet's amazement, Ivy practically melted. There was no mistaking the affection mingled with pride and fear in her eyes.

"I'll go with you." Will rose to his feet. "'Fear of man'—or woman in this case—'will prove to be a snare, but whoever trusts in the Lord is kept safe.' Proverbs 29:25."

Halston nodded approval. "Words of wisdom that we can take to heart. Shall we go visit the detective constable?"

Harriet started to rise too, but Ivy held up her palm. "Could you stay a while longer, Harriet? I'd appreciate your company."

"There don't seem to be any farm emergencies this evening," Harriet said. "I'd love to stay."

The men left, leaving Harriet and Ivy alone.

As soon as the front door closed, Harriet eyed Ivy. "He's the one, isn't he? The 'dear friend' you thought had written the note?"

The pink spots that appeared on Ivy's cheeks answered for her. "He brought me flowers the day after I came home from the hospital. I was too embarrassed at first to tell him about the note. He was embarrassed to tell me about his meeting with Heidi. But when I told him she'd been arrested, he told me he'd confronted her. And I showed him the note."

"What did he say?"

"That he wished he'd thought of such a rendezvous. One with a much happier ending."

Harriet grinned. "He said that?"

Ivy's tiny smile was both pleased and embarrassed. "It turned out to be a very pleasant evening for us."

"Until Will called?" Harriet guessed.

"We're both glad he did," Ivy said. "Hopefully, we can soon put this matter behind us."

"Then I'm glad too. One question though. How did you know I was with Will?"

"I didn't." Ivy chuckled. "That was a happy coincidence."

Indeed it was, Harriet mused as she finished her tea. She wouldn't have wanted to miss out on meeting Halston Dahlbury. "I'm glad you wanted me to come."

"You seem to have a knack for solving mysteries," Ivy said. "Sooner or later, you'll discover the identity of the ghost knight. I pray you stay safe while you're doing it."

"I'll be careful," Harriet assured her.

"I suppose you know Fern wrote the note."

"She told me. At least we know she wasn't the ghost knight."

"Only because she didn't think of it."

Harriet let the comment slide, guessing that the disgust in Ivy's voice hid the pain of betrayal she must be feeling.

Ivy had apparently tired of the conversation too. "Would you like another sandwich?" she asked with a bright smile.

"No, thank you." Harriet patted her stomach. "I've eaten enough for the evening."

"That's right. What did you have at the Crow's Nest?"

Harriet told Ivy about the different appetizers while helping her hostess clean up. Polly called while Harriet was drying the teapot with the news that Van had invited her on the whale-watching excursion for the next day. Though it was short notice, for which Polly profusely apologized, Harriet encouraged her to have a good time.

Naturally, Ivy wanted to know all the details. Harriet filled her in, which led to Ivy reminiscing about young men she'd dated in her youth. In swapping stories, they managed to steer clear of any talk of Fern or the ghost knight until Will and Halston returned.

"I told the DC my story," Halston said. "Then we went with him to Heidi's hotel. She's gone."

"What do you mean?" Ivy asked, her eyes wide. "How could she be gone?"

"I don't know, but she is," Will replied. "When she didn't answer the door, Van had the manager unlock it."

"Can he do that?" Harriet asked.

"As a DC, Van had a duty to ensure that she was okay," Will said. "Like Halston said, she was gone, and so was her luggage. Even the towels were gone."

The towels? People actually did that?

"I appear to be in good company," Will continued. "She left without paying her bill. My loss was nothing compared to the hotel's."

"Surely they have her credit card on file," Ivy protested.

"They do," Halston said. "But it must be maxed out, because the charge was denied. The manager filed a complaint with DC Worthington right then and there."

The two men seemed in remarkably good spirits, as if they'd returned from a grand adventure. Though they'd commiserated with the manager, they talked over each other as they shared additional details about their evening.

When it was time to go, Ivy's mood grew somber as she walked them to the door. "I can't help but worry what more Heidi might do. I heard she sometimes engages in shady practices, but I refused to believe what I thought was gossip. I considered Heidi a friend and her detractors to be jealous competitors. Now I'm sorry I didn't pay more attention to the rumors."

Will gave her a sympathetic smile. "Do you mind if I ask the names of these jealous competitors?"

Ivy let out a heavy sigh as her shoulders slumped. "Emma and Wes Brinley."

"Pot, meet kettle." Harriet clapped her hand over her mouth. "I didn't mean to say that."

"Too late now," Halston declared, though not unkindly. "I assume that's shorthand for the old expression about the pot calling the kettle black."

"You mean the Brinleys..." Ivy raised her eyes to the heavens and shook her head. "Why am I not surprised?"

Harriet put up her hands. "All I know is that someone told me Wes pretty much did to Heidi what Halston caught Heidi trying to do. Whether that's true or not, I can't say."

"And this someone was?" Ivy prompted.

With three sets of eyes on her and considering the other confidences that had been shared in good faith that evening—not counting Heidi's confession—Harriet felt compelled to tell them.

"Poppy Schofield." She bit her lip then said, "I believe her."

"And Wes had the nerve to accuse *me* of lying." Ivy seemed about to explode.

"That's the piece you wanted me to see," Halston said. "Maybe the pastor and I should go have a talk with him tonight too."

"Dress up as ghost knights, and you might scare a confession out of him," Ivy joked.

At least, Harriet hoped she was joking. The last thing the village needed was for the ghost knight to attack again.

CHAPTER SEVENTEEN

Harriet and Polly chose to eat lunch on Wednesday at a delicatessen with a well-deserved reputation for their quality meats and cheeses. However, the women's primary interest in the deli was its location across the street from Uniquities. Once their orders were ready, they carried their trays to a table beside the window.

Harriet opted for a cracked-pepper turkey sandwich with Havarti cheese on rosemary focaccia bread while Polly chose the Triple Threat—slices of smoked turkey, Black Forest ham, and roast beef with melted cheddar.

Real cheddar with a sharpness unlike any cheddar Harriet had ever purchased at an American supermarket. She'd quickly developed a taste for it, though her favorite remained the milder Havarti.

"Thanks for lunch," Polly said. Yesterday the streak in her hair had been a dynamic shade of gold, but now every single strand was ebony. A whim? Or a deliberate choice that reflected her mood? Harriet wasn't sure.

"It's the least I can do, since your plans were canceled."

"That wasn't your fault."

"I still feel responsible."

"Please don't. What's meant to be is meant to be."

Van had called Polly early that morning to say he had to work. Harriet wasn't surprised, since Heidi Paxton, charged with assault and now with fraud, had left her hotel without paying the bill. But she was still disappointed on Polly's behalf.

The burden of finding Heidi before the trail grew cold had fallen on Van's shoulders. He'd been promised Friday off instead, more to avoid paying him overtime than to make up for ruining his date, but Polly had given him no assurance of her own availability on that day. "As soon as I do," she'd said to Harriet when she unexpectedly showed up at the clinic that morning, "we'll have three farm calls and five emergencies."

Harriet thought her friend usually went with the flow about such things. Could it be that she was more eager to go out with Van than she wanted anyone to know?

Harriet bit into her sandwich and stared out the window. The sheet of plywood still covered the entrance to Uniquities. Someone had painted the word CLOSED in large red letters on the board.

"I wonder when they'll open again," Polly said. "Mum said she saw Wes and Emma at Galloway's General Store a couple days ago. He told her he felt fine, but Emma said he was under doctor's orders to get plenty of rest."

"I'm glad he's okay. Though I sure wish we knew how the attacker got out of Uniquities without being seen."

As Harriet took another bite of her sandwich, her gaze drifted to Mr. Calabash's insurance agency then to the Biscuit Bistro. "We should stop in and say hello to Poppy before we go back to the clinic."

"And pick up dessert." Polly's mood lifted. "I could eat a dozen of those pumpkin spice biscuits she sold at the festival. That'll make up for Van canceling on me."

"I can handle anything that might come up on Friday," Harriet said, trying to encourage her friend to take Van up on the possible reschedule.

Polly gave her a knowing look. "Does that mean you finished your speech for the women's luncheon?"

"Not quite," Harriet admitted. "I've been working on it though, and I'm sure I'll be prepared by Saturday."

"*If* you have time the next two days to work on it. Friday night is the auction, remember? You should be working on your talk now instead of treating me to a pity lunch."

"This is not a pity lunch, but a cheer-up lunch. I didn't want you to miss out on seeing the whales and the dolphins."

Polly's glum expression softened into regret. "I'm behaving like a brat, and I don't even know why." She offered a weak smile. "It's like I didn't know how much I wanted to go with Van until he canceled. I was more disappointed than I expected to be."

"Maybe you like him more than you realize," Harriet suggested.

"Maybe I do." Polly appeared reflective as she sipped her drink. "When we were paired to pick up contributions for the recent food drive, I got to know him in a different way. He's kind and warm and funny." She tilted her head in thought. "I was looking forward to seeing the whales too. But I think I'd feel this dejected no matter what we'd planned to do."

"As he hoped you would."

Polly gave her a quizzical glance then her eyes brightened. "He did say that, didn't he? He was right. And so are you. I *do* like him."

Harriet smiled. The rain cloud over Polly's ebony head had vanished, and Harriet couldn't help wondering if the gold streak would be back tomorrow.

She returned her gaze to the single-story shops on the other side of the narrow cobblestone street. It was such an interesting collection of businesses. Uniquities, an insurance agency, a bakery specializing in cookies, a dry cleaner, a fabric shop. That must be the one owned by Aunt Jinny's friend.

Harriet froze with a chip halfway to her mouth.

"What is it?" Polly asked.

"The shops."

Polly stared out the window. "What about them?"

"Don't you see?" Harriet dropped the chip onto her plate. "Uniquities isn't the only shop with a locked-room mystery. Mr. Calabash, Poppy, the fabric shop. Someone broke into each of them without leaving a trace of how they got in."

"You're right." Polly shifted in her seat to get a better view out the window.

"Remember last month when we thought Rowena's kidnappers might have secreted her away through the tunnel the smugglers used to use? Is it possible there's a tunnel under those shops too?"

"I wouldn't think so." Polly's mouth twisted into a doubtful frown. "Though I suppose anything is possible. But wouldn't the owners know if there was a tunnel under their shops?"

"Maybe. Maybe not," Harriet said. "But if there is a tunnel, and that's how the ghost knight got away, there's an entrance to the tunnel somewhere in those shops. And we're going to find it."

The afternoon sped by with enough appointments to leave no time for thinking about secret tunnels. It was well known in White Church Bay lore that eighteenth-century smugglers once used another of the seaside caves to hide such luxury goods as silks and teas from the customs officers. The tunnels, which connected to various houses along the slope, allowed the villagers to clandestinely move their products from the sea to the top of the hill without ever going outside.

Though the clinic's official closing time was four o'clock, it was closer to four thirty when the last patient, a rambunctious terrier, hopped and skipped out on three legs, since the fourth was bandaged due to an unfortunate encounter with a very angry cow. Another half an hour passed while Harriet prepped the examination rooms for the next day, tended to Maxwell and Charlie, changed clothes, and plopped down in the reading nook with a cup of tea.

She hadn't come into the tiny room to read, however. She was there to think.

The attacks on Ivy and Wes had driven the pranks and petty thefts from her mind. But what if they were somehow related? What if the ghost knight had moved around Mr. Calabash's pictures, and stolen Poppy's cookie jar? Had played the pranks in the fabric shop?

Perhaps the ghost knight had even stolen the *Three Dogs at Night* sculpture, which was why Wes thought Emma had already given it to Ivy. Since Ivy had still been upset the previous night about Wes accusing her of lying, he apparently hadn't apologized for his behavior even though he'd had plenty of time to ask Emma what had happened to the sculpture.

Maybe I should talk to Emma.

Harriet recalled how dismissive Emma had been of Ivy's and Wes's accounts of seeing the ghost knight. Not only did she not believe them, but she had accused them of making up the story to gain attention or, in Wes's case, to avoid admitting his clumsiness. Harriet had been irked by Emma's lack of compassion at the hospital, and she was even more irked as she recounted their conversation now.

"Maybe I should ask Van to talk to Emma," Harriet murmured to Maxwell, who rested on a plush cushion in front of the long window. A weak beam from the late afternoon sun bathed the dachshund in a pale rectangle of light. He raised his head when Harriet spoke. Then he yawned and nestled his long nose on his crossed paws once again.

"Or maybe I'm trying to find connections that don't exist."

She raised her arms above her head to ease the tension in her shoulders and shifted as the ache eased into her lower back. Lately she'd been doing too much standing and too much sitting. A long ramble was what she needed.

A few moments later, she was out the door with her jacket buttoned up and her wellies on her feet. She took the public path that ran parallel to the North Sea, but after a half mile or so, she veered slightly inland on a narrow path she'd never taken before. Could this have been the track Heidi had followed to Cobble Hill Farm?

If so, then Harriet should eventually end up at the public meadow where the festival had been held. However, she intended on walking only a few more minutes before turning back. The sky had darkened in the west, and the sun hung low. She didn't want to get caught in a rainstorm or lose her way in the dark.

The path skirted the edges of a narrow woods, at times meandering through the deciduous trees. Occasionally, Harriet glimpsed rural countryside on the other side of the woods or heard the quiet hum of an engine on a nearby road.

Other than that, the lone sounds were the distant roar of waves crashing against unseen cliff walls, the end-of-day songs of birds who hadn't yet flown south, and the blending chatter of woodland creatures.

As she sauntered along, her thoughts shifted to the legend of the lost drummer boy. The cave where Ivy had been attacked couldn't be too far away, at least not as the crow flew. If the legend had taken place here instead of Richmond, the little guy might have beaten his drum along a dark passageway leading from the cave to the village. To Uniquities or to Biscuit Bistro. An insurance agency or a fabric store.

Harriet could almost imagine the drumbeat.

The path took a sharp turn into the woods. Five or six steps later, Harriet suddenly stopped, shocked by the scene in front of her.

Fern Chapman, perched on a huge stump, was enclosed in the tight embrace of a sixtyish man wearing a plaid deerstalker cap. Neither seemed aware of Harriet's presence.

As she turned to go, she stepped on a twig that cracked like thunder. She grimaced but only hesitated a second before retracing her steps.

A second too long.

"Harriet Bailey?" Fern's shrill voice silenced the chatter of the wood's tiny animals and the songs of the birds. "There's no need to run away like an embarrassed schoolgirl."

Harriet slowly faced them, though she was tempted to shut her eyes. Fern, still sitting on the stump, held the man's arm. His plump cheeks were a deep red above a brush of a moustache and trimmed goatee.

"What are you doing wandering these woods?" Fern demanded. "You couldn't have known I'd be out here."

"I'm simply taking a walk."

"On my land? You can see my farm right over there." Fern pointed to the west. "I suppose Ivy sent you."

Harriet plunged her fists into her pockets. "Sent me to do what?"

"Spy on me. On us."

"Why would I do that?" *And why didn't I stay home with Maxwell and Charlie?*

Fern's beau—or whoever he was—managed to extricate himself and took a couple steps forward. Harriet stood her ground. Could this unlikely couple be a ghost knight team? Fern had already admitted to writing the note that lured Ivy to the cave. What if this man had been waiting there?

"We haven't met," the stranger said. "I'm Lenton Mutter. Perhaps you've heard the name?"

Harriet quickly flipped through a mental list of people she'd met or read about in the *Whitby Gazette*, the local weekly newspaper, since moving to Yorkshire. "I don't believe I have." She managed to keep her tone cordial despite her wariness. "I'm Harriet Bailey."

"He knows that," Fern snapped. She linked her arm through Mr. Mutter's and graced him with a smile.

Harriet couldn't help herself. Her heart melted at the loving look Mr. Mutter bestowed on Fern in return.

He faced Harriet again. "It is a pleasure to meet you, Dr. Bailey, though I do regret the odd circumstances. Miss Chapman and I find it prudent to court in secret."

"Because of Ivy?" Surely she didn't care who Fern dated. Though given the sisters' rivalry, maybe she would. Except now that she was—well, Harriet wasn't sure what the relationship was between Ivy and Halston Dahlbury. They probably weren't sure themselves.

"I don't wish to tell Ivy yet," Fern said. "She'll be so jealous, and I don't want to do that to her. But it's Lenton's children who must absolutely be kept in the dark. They'd be furious if they knew." She lowered her voice to a stage-whisper. "He's very rich."

Fern's furtive expression caused Harriet to suspect the older woman would enjoy nothing more than for the secret to get out. Nor did Harriet believe Fern cared about Ivy's feelings. After all, she had written the note impersonating Halston and inviting Ivy to the rendezvous in the cave, so she knew there was something going on between him and her sister. Her concern simply added to the drama she enjoyed so much.

"Fernie exaggerates," Lenton said, his tone indulgent.

Fernie? For the second time, Harriet wished she was home alone with a compelling novel, a cup of tea, and her two furry companions.

"The Mutter family fortune is far from what it once was," he continued. "I'm the second son of a second son of a second son." He raised his hands in a helpless gesture. "Not that the first son of the first son of the first son has fared much better. Even so, my children are not eager to acquire a stepmother."

"I imagine that can be difficult."

"They're as old as you," Fern said, rolling her eyes. "They need to accept that Lenton is still an attractive man."

The sky darkened, and Harriet glanced skyward. A cloud momentarily hid the sun, and a clap of thunder sounded in the distance.

"I should get home before the rain gets here," Harriet said, thankful the impending storm gave her an excuse to get away from these two. "It was nice meeting you, Mr. Mutter."

"Wait a minute." Fern came closer and, for once, her over-the-top persona had disappeared. "Is it true that Heidi Paxton is the ghost knight?"

Harriet hesitated before answering. She wanted to set the record straight, but she didn't want to engage in gossip. Especially not with Fern.

"Heidi didn't attack Wes. She has an alibi."

"What about Ivy?"

"She had an explanation for her whereabouts."

"But no alibi."

"No."

"I was with Lenton when Ivy went to the cave. We were behind one of the booths for a few stolen moments together before I was forced to take Ivy's place on the stage." Fern lowered her gaze and let out a sigh. "I never meant for her to get hurt. Or Wes either."

"I'm sure you didn't." *Though you didn't seem to care much either.* It was an ugly thought, but Harriet couldn't help recalling how bothered she'd been by Fern's indifference toward her sister.

Fern suddenly emitted a sharp, ironic laugh. "I was with Lenton when Wes was attacked too. If I'd been a suspect, he'd have been my alibi. No more secret courtship."

"I guess it's a good thing then that you weren't a suspect." *Though you might be one now.*

"I was on my way home when Emma passed me," Fern continued, as if Harriet hadn't spoken. "Of course, I didn't know what had happened to Wes, but Emma must have gotten the news right about then. She made a U-turn and sped toward Whitby."

How strange. Harriet was almost certain that Emma had told Van she was at home when he called to tell her about Wes. Why would she lie?

Harriet stared at Fern and Lenton, who were making what she could only describe as goo-goo eyes at each other. Her mind raced. Fern and Lenton were each other's alibi for both attacks. Was the relationship between the Chapman sisters so strained that Fern, who reveled in drama, would do something so awful?

A shiver raced down Harriet's spine as she turned to head home.

CHAPTER EIGHTEEN

The clinic phone rang Thursday morning before Harriet had a chance to unlock the front door. Polly wouldn't be in for another hour, so Harriet answered the phone while booting up the office computer.

"Morning, Doctor," a male voice replied to her standard greeting. "This is Andrew Ellsworth calling. The rumor around town is that you were at the pavilion when DC Worthington found that tunic in a bin belonging to Heidi Paxton."

"That's right." Harriet's nerves tingled, though she couldn't pinpoint why. But it seemed odd that Andrew would want to talk to her about the costume. Especially since he probably didn't like her very much after their visit the other day. Perhaps she should have called to let him know Jane Birtwhistle had confirmed his alibi.

On second thought, the fact that she had checked his alibi rather than taking him at his word about it might have strained their relationship even more.

"The detective constable had me come to the station to identify it if I could." A heavy sigh came through the line. "It's mine, all right."

Harriet wondered if he'd fainted at the sight of the bloodstain but decided not to bring that up. "Are you certain it's yours?"

"I had a personalized name tag sewn into the collar, and that's been cut out. But yes, it's mine. I accidentally ripped the lining once, and my wife fixed it for me. She's handy with a needle, but the repair is obvious if you know what you're looking for."

"What did Van say when you told him it was yours?"

"He knows I didn't attack Miss Ivy in that cave." Andrew's tone sounded close to a challenge.

"I know that too," Harriet replied evenly. "And I don't believe you attacked Wes either."

"That's much appreciated. I'm glad to hear you say it." He hesitated. "I don't know how or why Heidi had my tunic. But I wanted to let you know that my wife went to the dry cleaner to pick up the costume before she left for Birmingham. Preston Cooper, the manager, couldn't find it. He checked all the racks."

"So it was stolen."

"He didn't want to admit that possibility, but he said strange things had been going on there. He even joked to my wife that elves came out at night to cause mischief."

First a ghost soldier and now elves.

In reality, a very human person who'd progressed from mischief to thievery to assault.

"Is this the dry cleaner located between the Biscuit Bistro and a fabric shop?" Harriet asked.

"Sure is. Why do you ask?"

"From what I've heard, other stores on that street have elves too," Harriet said lightly.

"Is that a fact?"

"From what I've heard," she repeated, hoping he wouldn't ask her for any details. Poppy had mentioned asking Van to get the business owners together for a meeting. Harriet would like to be a fly on the wall when or if that happened.

"No sign of how someone could have gotten into the stores?" he asked.

"There doesn't seem to be."

Andrew's tone lowered as if he were speaking to himself instead of Harriet. "Like at Uniquities when Wes was attacked. I wonder…" he began, then his voice faded away.

Once again, Harriet's nerves tingled. "Wonder what?" she prompted.

"It's probably nothing. But do you know about the smuggling tunnels? They're certainly no secret."

"Polly Thatcher and I were talking about them yesterday." Harriet's voice rose with excitement. "Do you think there could be another one? A secret tunnel that's been forgotten?"

"Seems hard to believe," Andrew admitted. "But the DC told me he can't figure out how Ivy's ghost knight disappeared. He and a few others went as far back into the cave as they could without finding another way to get out. But whoever wore my tunic didn't walk through a wall or disappear into thin air."

"I agree."

The clinic door opened, and Aunt Jinny walked in with a bakery box. Harriet held a finger to her lips.

"Do you have time today for a little expedition?" Andrew asked.

Now the nerves on Harriet's nerves were tingling. "You want to go to the cave?"

"It was one of my favorite places to explore when I was a lad. Maybe I'll see something Van missed."

The thought of descending that cliff slope again was daunting, but Harriet had done it once before. She could do it again. "We should ask Van to join us. My aunt Jinny just walked in. I'd like her to come too."

"The four of us then," Andrew agreed. "But no one else. We don't want the ghost knight to know we're headed to his lair."

Harriet couldn't help but smile at Andrew's melodramatic choice of words and his equally melodramatic tone. "Agreed."

"What time?"

Harriet consulted her appointment calendar and an intrigued Aunt Jinny to come up with a couple afternoon options for Andrew to give Van.

As soon as the call ended, Aunt Jinny opened the bakery box to reveal half a dozen assorted doughnuts. "What was that all about?"

Instead of answering, Harriet gestured toward the box. "You've already been to the village this morning?"

"Since the wee hours. A tourist lost control of his vehicle out on the old cliff road around midnight. His family seems to be okay except for aches and bruises. But he was seriously injured."

"I'm so sorry," Harriet said. "That poor family."

"We got them settled into the hotel a couple of hours ago, but I doubt they'll get much sleep."

"And what about you?"

"I'm headed home after we've had a bit of a catch-up." She pretended to glare at Harriet. "Now what's all this about going to the cave with Andrew Ellsworth?"

When they gathered at the cave entrance after the clinic closed that afternoon, the group included two additional members—Polly, who now sported a vibrant blue streak in her dark hair, and Will. Polly had taken Andrew's message confirming that Van would join them for the excursion.

Andrew couldn't fault Harriet for letting Polly tag along, since he'd impulsively invited Will when he ran into him at the hardware store. He'd bought five headlamps, and Aunt Jinny had found a couple in her utility room, so they had an extra. Andrew and Van also carried high-powered flashlights.

Once everyone had pulled on their wellies, which were great for walking in water but not all that safe for descending the cliff slope, Andrew led the way along one of the ledges bordering the channel of water into the darkness of the cave.

"This is where we found Ivy and Jiffy," Aunt Jinny said when they reached the spot. "Are we sure there isn't someplace where the ghost knight could have hidden until we left?"

"I considered that," Van said. Since this wasn't an official search, he was casually dressed in jeans and a faded sweatshirt. "I checked when I brought the team back the day after her attack. If such a spot exists, we all missed it."

Andrew slowly swept his flashlight beam across the stone wall. "Wish I'd been able to come with you then." He sounded a little miffed that Van hadn't asked him to join that search. If Van noticed, he chose to ignore the subtle rebuke.

The water channel gently curved, and the channel widened until the ledges were nonexistent. They sloshed through shallow water, Andrew still in the lead and Will bringing up the rear.

When they reached a fork, Andrew stopped and waited for everyone to catch up. "That direction leads to a cavern," he said, sweeping the flashlight beam. "That's a dead end, so we'll go this way."

"I had no idea this tunnel went so far," Will said to Harriet as they followed Andrew around another bend. "Thankfully there aren't other passageways, or we might get lost trying to get back out."

"Someone should have stayed at the entrance to watch for the ghost knight to come out after Miss Ivy's attack." Andrew's sharp tone surprised Harriet. She exchanged a glance with Will, who shrugged. Apparently, Andrew was truly upset that Van hadn't included him in the prior search of the cave.

"Whoever it was could have stayed back here until the coast was clear," Andrew continued. "He didn't even need to hide."

"You're right, Andrew," Aunt Jinny said, her voice calm and without a hint of reproach. "We were too focused on taking care of Ivy and Jiffy to give much thought to their attacker."

For a moment, the cave was silent except for the quiet lapping of the sea water against the stone walls. Then Andrew spoke again, his voice gruff yet apologetic. "As was right. They needed help, and I'm glad you and Harriet were there to give it."

Harriet inwardly smiled. How she wished she had Aunt Jinny's knack for defusing such situations with grace and dignity.

Polly, who was walking beside Van and in front of Harriet, suddenly stumbled.

Van caught her around the waist before she fell into the water.

She clutched his arms as she tried to steady herself.

"What happened?" he asked as the others gathered around him and Polly.

"My ankle." Polly grimaced. "I think I twisted it."

Aunt Jinny took Polly's arm to help her balance. "Can you put any weight on it?"

Polly's gray eyes glistened, but she gamely held back her tears as she tried—and failed—to stand on her own. "How could I have been so clumsy?"

"You're never clumsy."

At Van's earnest tone, Harriet and Aunt Jinny exchanged amused glances.

"I slipped on a rock." Polly shrugged as she stood on one leg. Water dripped from her upraised boot.

"We need to go back," Van said.

"We can't," Andrew protested.

Van's eyes flashed with rare irritation. "Dr. Garrett can't examine her in here."

"Gentlemen." Will lifted his hands in a conciliatory manner. "We don't all have to go, and we don't all have to stay."

"Will's right," Aunt Jinny said. "He and I can take Polly to my office while the rest of you explore the cave."

Van opened then closed his mouth, his expression as downcast as Harriet had ever seen it. He was obviously torn between his desire to assist Polly and his duty to locate a possible escape route. The frown on Polly's face led Harriet to believe that she didn't appreciate the suggestion either.

"Or Will could stay, and Van and I could take you back, Polly," Aunt Jinny suggested.

"That sounds fine," Polly said. She smiled sweetly at Van, who seemed much happier than he'd been mere seconds before.

"It's settled then," Andrew said. "Is it okay with you, Dr. Garrett, if we all meet up at the dower cottage when we're done here?"

Aunt Jinny gave him a warm smile. "I'll have the kettle on."

"Maybe I should go with you too," Harriet offered. "You might need my help going back up the cliff path. Skippy isn't here to call in a helicopter rescue."

"I'll get a boat to pick us up and take us around to the dock," Van said. "We'll manage."

Aunt Jinny squeezed Harriet's arm. "Stay with Will and Andrew. You don't want to miss this adventure."

"You're right," Harriet admitted. She'd be disappointed if Will and Andrew found another way out of the cave without her.

Aunt Jinny and Van, supporting Polly between them, slowly walked toward the cave's entrance.

"Let's keep going," Andrew said. "If we don't find an exit, we'll want to climb up the cliff path before the sun sets. Even with torches, that route can be tricky in the dark." Since the carnival was gone, they'd driven across the meadow and parked their vehicles near the top of the path.

The trio waded about a minute longer. The water level lowered until it barely covered the soles of their wellies. The tunnel took two sharp bends, one immediately after the other, and was so narrow they were forced to walk single file.

"I remember this." Andrew glanced over his shoulder at Harriet and Will. "There's another bend, and then the tunnel starts to slope upward. That's as far as my friends and I ever went."

They rounded the corner—only to be faced with a rock wall about seven feet high.

"This isn't right," Andrew said, obviously puzzled. "This can't be right."

"How long has it been since you were here last?" Will asked.

Andrew shrugged as he moved his flashlight beam over the huge stones blocking the way. "Fifteen years or so. This wall wasn't here back then."

"Memory can be a funny thing," Will said. "Fifteen years is a long time."

"Maybe you're mistaken and this is as far as you got back then," Harriet added.

"I'm not wrong." Andrew raised his beam to the ceiling. "See the gap up there? The tunnel continues on the other side."

"We can't crawl through that gap," Harriet said. "Even if we wanted to, we couldn't get up there."

Andrew scrutinized the wall. "This is all wrong. See this sediment?" He ran his hand over a few of the stones. "These were in mud or water, and not that long ago. These rocks were moved here recently to block the tunnel. Not years ago."

"By the ghost knight?" Harriet asked.

Andrew shrugged. "By someone." He knelt and examined the lower section of the wall. "This is interesting."

Harriet bent, hands on her knees. Her headlamp illuminated a haphazard pile of rocks. At least, that was all she could see.

"Watch your step," Andrew cautioned as he pointed his flashlight to the base of the pile. "These rocks are loose. I think they can be moved without bringing down the wall."

"Do you mean you want to play Jenga with this wall?" Will asked incredulously.

"I think that would be a really bad idea," Harriet said.

"Look." Andrew stood and faced them. "You two step back. I'm going to move these rocks and see what happens." He pointed to the rocks in the bottom corner.

"What will happen is a rockslide," Will insisted. "It's too dangerous."

"I don't think so."

"Maybe we should find someone who's an expert with this kind of thing," Will said. "That wall will still be there tomorrow."

To Harriet's surprise, Andrew agreed. "You're right. It will be. But what if the ghost knight attacks someone else tonight? This is our chance to find out who's besmirching the sterling reputation of King Arthur's chivalrous knights."

Will seemed at a loss for words after Andrew's odd little speech, and Harriet couldn't blame him. She shared Will's concern, but Andrew had made an excellent point.

"I never thought of it that way," she said to him. "Someone steals your costume and then behaves abominably. Not at all like a true knight."

"You're making fun of me." Andrew ducked his head. "I guess I do get carried away sometimes."

"No, I'm not." Harriet touched his arm. "This person needs to be caught, but we can't let ourselves get trapped down here. It's time we go. Like Will said, we can return tomorrow."

"Besides," Will added, "it's getting late, and we still need to get back up the cliff path."

Andrew heaved a deep sigh. "All right. Let's go. Will, you can lead the way."

Will headed back the way they'd come, with Harriet following behind him.

Andrew trailed her for several feet then suddenly turned, raced to the pile of rocks, and started pulling out the bottom ones.

"Andrew, no!" Harriet started after him, but Will grabbed her arm.

He pointed the flashlight at Andrew and the wall. The rocks hadn't moved, but a rough square now appeared in the bottom corner.

"It's a kind of door." Andrew examined the next section of rocks and pulled out a few more. The square enlarged.

Will stepped in front of Harriet so he could examine the pile. "Why aren't they falling?"

"It's the way they've been wedged together," Andrew explained. "It's honestly brilliant."

Will aimed the flashlight beam into the space. "The tunnel slopes upward, like you said."

"May I see?" Harriet asked.

"Sure." Will and Andrew moved to make way for her, and Will gave her the flashlight. "Be careful," he warned as she crouched to get a better look.

She focused the beam on the floor and followed it as far as the light reached. The slope was gentle and appeared to curve. She aimed the beam at the roof, about seven or eight feet above the floor. The beam slid down the far wall to the path then past a dark object.

"Something's in there," she said, barely able to contain her excitement. "I think it's a blue tarp."

Harriet shivered, everything within her urging her to retrieve whatever was beneath the tarp.

Behind her, Will and Andrew clamored to see inside the gap, but Harriet ignored them. She eyed the opening, assessing whether she could get through it, and decided she could. A second before she started through, an image of the lost drummer boy flashed in her mind. He'd been lowered into a tunnel and was never seen again.

Will and Andrew wouldn't let that happen to her, but neither would they understand why she had to go through the gap. She set aside the flashlight, since her headlamp provided all the light she needed, then quickly scurried through.

Someone grabbed at her boots, but she slipped free and a moment later was on the other side.

"Harriet." Will shone the flashlight into the gap. "Come back here. It's not safe."

"In a moment." The damp cave floor soaked her pant legs as she crawled toward the tarp. "Pray there aren't any bugs."

"Or mice," Andrew called in a surprisingly positive tone. Though perhaps his good humor wasn't all that much of a surprise. He was probably thrilled that Harriet had been the one to take the risk.

"Thanks a lot, Andrew," she called back sarcastically. From behind her, the flashlight cast a bright light. Probably Will keeping a close eye on her. She stood and adjusted her headlamp to peer past the tunnel's curve. The slope stretched up as far as the light reached. Could the exit be near or even in the village?

"Harriet, please." Will's tone wasn't nearly as jovial as Andrew's had been.

Harriet studied the tarp. "I don't think this has been here long. It's relatively clean."

"Please grab whatever it is and get back here," Will said.

Taking a deep breath, she gingerly pinched one corner of the tarp between her thumb and index finger and uncovered a large metal box with a silver hasp. As she opened the lid and looked inside, she gasped.

Inside the box was the *Three Dogs at Night* bronze sculpture.

CHAPTER NINETEEN

As promised, by the time Harriet, Will, and Andrew arrived at the dower cottage, Aunt Jinny had an urn of steaming water on her sideboard, along with a single-serve coffee machine, assorted sandwiches, and a veggie platter. Harriet had called her aunt from the Beast to let her know they were on their way, after a quick detour to their respective homes to clean up.

Van and Polly, her wrapped ankle propped on a pillow on the coffee table, sat on the sofa. The others arranged chairs in a semicircle around the table. In the middle, on top of the metal box, was the bronze sculpture of three Labrador retrievers playing beside a tree. The moon was visible through its outstretched limbs.

Van had put on gloves to remove the sculpture from the box but hadn't allowed anyone else to touch it. He'd phoned Detective Inspector Kerry McCormick at county HQ about the find. She'd agreed that Van could take the sculpture to the crime lab first thing in the morning.

While they ate their sandwiches, Andrew shared how they'd found the pile of rocks blocking the tunnel's path, and Harriet explained how she'd found the missing sculpture.

"As far as we know," she said, "the three people involved with the sculpture are Ivy, Wes, and Emma. Ivy wanted to show the piece to Halston Dahlbury. She was upset when Wes showed up at the pavilion without it, and they argued."

"Because Wes said Emma had already given it to Ivy. He accused Ivy of lying," Aunt Jinny added. "He even accused her of stealing it."

"Does anyone here honestly believe that Ivy went to the cave to hide the sculpture?" Will's skeptical tone indicated his own answer. "Then happened to be attacked by someone else in the cave?"

"Which means Emma and Wes are the most logical ones to have hidden the sculpture," Van said.

"Wes did it," Andrew said. "He was already mad at Ivy for questioning him. He must have stolen my costume from the dry cleaner. It's a couple doors down from Uniquities. Then he disguised himself as the ghost knight and attacked Miss Ivy. And we all know what happened after that. He conked his own head to divert attention from himself. Even Emma's been going around saying so."

Will's mouth quirked. "She told Harriet and me that at hospital, though she suggested that it was clumsiness."

"Wes isn't guilty simply because we want him to be." Despite using the word *we*, Aunt Jinny directed her comment to Andrew. "We can't allow our own dislike for someone to cloud our judgment."

Polly shifted toward Van and touched his arm. "You and Harriet were there. Do you think Wes intentionally hurt himself?"

"I don't think it's likely. Though I also don't know how the attacker got away when all the doors were secured from the inside." Van peered across the table at Harriet. "What's your opinion?"

Ever since she'd found the sculpture, Harriet had been reviewing every tidbit of information she'd gathered over the past few days. Her conclusions were still mostly conjecture, but they were based on her instincts and judgment. Though she still had unanswered questions, a plausible scenario had begun to form in her mind.

"I'm one hundred percent certain Wes wasn't the one who attacked Ivy," Harriet said. "I saw his arms when he was unconscious. He had no marks or bruising where Jiffy would have grabbed him. And I'm confident his wound wasn't self-inflicted. But that doesn't mean his fall wasn't an accident."

Will blinked in surprise. "You mean he knew who attacked him."

"I think so, yes."

"And never said."

"Right." Harriet slid a baby carrot through the pool of dip on her plate. "Family loyalties can be very strong. Even when family members bicker."

"Emma," several voices said at the same time, some with certainty and others as a question.

"When we saw her at the hospital, she said she was home when Van called to tell her about Wes," Harriet said. "But Fern told me yesterday that she was driving home from Whitby about that same time and Emma sped around her. Then Emma made a U-turn and drove back toward Whitby."

"She lied to me," Van said, obviously offended.

"That doesn't make her guilty," Andrew responded. "Remember what Dr. Garrett said about our judgment being clouded."

Will stared at the heavy sculpture. "Let's circle back to Emma telling Wes she'd given the *Three Dogs* to Ivy when she hadn't. Poppy Schofield, a woman of reputable standing, has accused Wes of dishonest business practices. Maybe he's not the only dishonest Brinley."

"I wonder where we could find Sir Halston Dahlbury at this time of the evening?" Aunt Jinny mused as she reached for her phone. "Ivy wanted him to see this specific piece. Perhaps we should give him that opportunity."

"Who are you calling?" Harriet asked with an amused smile.

Aunt Jinny held up one finger. "Hello, Ivy. I wonder if you could do me a little favor."

Ivy and Halston arrived about half an hour later, and the story of how the *Three Dogs at Night* sculpture had been found was told once again. Ivy also made an appropriate fuss over Polly's hurt ankle.

Afterward, Ivy told the group how Queen Elizabeth II herself had knighted Halston for his scholarship pertaining to Great Britain's seventeenth-century artistic heritage. He was also a self-taught expert on Alistair Artemis, the purported creator of the piece. It was why Ivy had been so eager to have *Three Dogs at Night* on display at the antiques exhibit. And, she admitted, for Halston to see such a rare find.

Sir Halston put on gloves and examined the sculpture with great care. He even pulled a jeweler's loupe from his pocket.

"Wes seemed excited to get a knowledgeable valuation," Ivy said while he worked. "In retrospect, I think he was surprised I didn't have the sculpture on display. But I regrettably lost my temper, and he understandably became defensive. It was a sorry matter all the way around."

Aunt Jinny patted Ivy's hand. "And a very unfortunate one. Hopefully the entire mystery will soon be solved."

"I hope that too. Halston, what can you tell us about this piece?"

"It's handsome work, isn't it?" he said. "The artist should have been proud to put his own name on it instead of attributing it to someone whose work is superior."

"Just to be clear," Van said, "you're saying this sculpture is a forgery?"

"Based on a few telltale signs, yes. For example, the maker's stamp on the bottom is muddied. And the etchings on the tree bark lack the attention to detail one would expect from a genuine Artemis. The forger is skilled though, so this piece does have some value."

"Emma must have known it wasn't real," Ivy said. "That was why she didn't want you to see it. She'd be exposed as a fraud, as Heidi has been."

"I don't think it's too much of a leap to suspect that Emma is dressing up as the ghost knight," Van said. "She should be detained before word gets around that the sculpture is no longer in the cave."

"Perhaps letting it be known we found the sculpture is exactly what we should do," Harriet suggested. "After all, what evidence do you have against her? No more than before we found the *Three Dogs*. But what if we schedule a special showing of the sculpture at the pavilion tomorrow afternoon, before the Antique Festival auction, and make a point of inviting Wes and Emma? They'd be too curious not to come."

Van frowned in puzzlement. "What will that prove?"

"Maybe nothing." Harriet smiled. "But I have a little surprise in mind that could reveal the ghost knight's true identity."

CHAPTER TWENTY

The plans that had been finalized the night before were cleared with DI McCormick and then set in motion. First thing Friday morning, Ivy arranged for the few people on the guest list to receive their invitations to the afternoon event where Sir Halston Dahlbury would unveil a recently discovered antique to the exclusive group.

Aunt Jinny and Ivy, ever the consummate hostesses, greeted the invited guests when they arrived at the pavilion and ushered them to a sectioned-off corner of the large room where Will and Andrew had arranged chairs in a U-shape in front of a display pedestal. *Three Dogs at Night* was covered by a large box. Both the sculpture and the metal had been dusted for prints earlier in the day, but the crime tech found only smudges.

Now the two men, along with Sir Halston, welcomed the other guests while Polly, ignoring Aunt Jinny's strict orders to stay off her foot, presided over the punch table.

Harriet and Van peered through the gaps of a curtained screen as Mr. Calabash, Poppy Schofield, Preston Cooper who managed the dry cleaner, and Ruby Corbin who owned the fabric store enjoyed punch and biscuits as they mingled.

Last to arrive were the Brinley cousins, Wes and Emma. Like the other guests, they'd dressed up for the occasion. Wes wore pressed trousers with a button-down shirt and tie beneath a blazer, which complemented Emma's stylish burgundy dress with its long sleeves and flared skirt.

"I was worried they weren't going to come," Harriet whispered to Van.

"Yesterday you said they'd be too curious not to," Van replied.

"That was more hopeful thinking than anything else," Harriet admitted as she tugged at the hem of her suit jacket. "Now that everyone's here, we might as well begin. You know what to do."

"We'll be waiting for our cue."

Van disappeared down a corridor, and Harriet approached the group. She caught Ivy's gaze and dipped her head in a brief nod. Ivy went to the display pedestal and rang a tiny silver bell. The murmuring conversations around her faded away.

"It's time to begin," she said, smiling broadly and extending her arms in welcome. "Please take your seats, everyone. Sir Halston, would you join me here at the front?"

Harriet sat beside Andrew in a chair that allowed her to see the curtained partition. Which meant Van, once he returned from the meeting room where Harriet had hidden her surprise, could see her without being seen himself.

As they'd planned, Aunt Jinny and Will managed to maneuver Wes and Emma into two of the seats at the bottom of the U. It wasn't that difficult, since neither Andrew nor Poppy wanted to be anywhere near the cousins. With the wall behind them and chairs lined up on either side, neither Wes nor Emma could easily leave the space.

Ivy formally introduced her "dear friend," extolling his many accomplishments in a voice filled with pride. Harriet barely listened as she cast surreptitious glances toward Emma, who sat between Wes and Will. Though he slouched in his seat, Wes appeared tense with his mouth set in a grim line and his jaw clenched. He focused his gaze on the display pedestal, no doubt concerned at what was beneath the box.

Was he wondering if the missing sculpture was still in the cave? Or was he unaware that it had ever been there?

In sharp contrast, Emma appeared bored and as if she didn't have a care in the world. She crossed her legs, first one way and then the other, examined her glittering manicure, and played with the multiple bracelets on her wrist. Harriet doubted that Emma heard a word of Ivy's introduction.

"Now it's time," Ivy said, her voice rising with enthusiasm, "to uncover the sculpture found yesterday evening by our own Dr. Harriet Bailey as she, along with Pastor Will Knight and Andrew Ellsworth, explored the pirates' cave. The very same cave where I was attacked by the ghost knight."

As she spoke, Wes sat forward as if poised to leap from his seat. One hand rested against his chest while the other gripped his knee.

Emma glared at Ivy from beneath her heavily made-up eyes.

If looks could kill...

"Halston," Ivy said, turning toward him, "would you do the honors?"

"It would be my pleasure." He stationed himself behind the pedestal and placed his hands on either side of the box. "Ladies and gentlemen," he intoned in his distinguished accent, "may I present a bronze sculpture that is a lovely piece but, I regret to say, is not Alistair Artemis's lost *Three Dogs at Night*."

As he lifted the lid, Harriet stood, and Van appeared from behind the partition and joined Halston at the pedestal.

Ivy turned her gaze to Wes and Emma. "I saw this very same sculpture in Uniquities a few weeks ago and asked Wes to let us display it during the festival exhibit. I'm sorry to say we had a misunderstanding." She offered him an apologetic smile. "I didn't lie to you. And I didn't steal it from you." Her eyes glistened with amusement as she chuckled. "I certainly didn't hide it behind a pile of rocks in the cave. But I think you know who did."

Wes opened his mouth, but no words came out. "Emma told me—"

Emma grabbed Wes's arm. "Will you be quiet?" She addressed Ivy. "We all heard your so-called expert say this"—she waved her hand toward the pedestal—"*thing* isn't a genuine Artemis. Whereas the bronze you saw in Uniquities most definitely was, and now it's missing."

Harriet had to admit that was an interesting strategy.

Emma stood and announced to the group, "This is nothing more than an elaborate plot to hide Ivy Chapman's wrongdoing. At best, she handled our authentic Artemis with negligence and somehow lost it. At worst, she gave our invaluable bronze to her boyfriend, and they're trying to cheat Wes and me with this replica."

Sir Halston bristled. "None of what you say is true, young lady."

Emma folded her arms and shot him a close-mouthed smile. Then she said, "You deny my story, and I deny yours. We're at an impasse, old man."

Wes stood beside her, fear in his eyes. "We should leave," he said, his tone wary.

"No one is going anywhere," Van said. "You're absolutely right, Ms. Brinley. As far as the bronze sculpture is concerned, no one here can prove that you or your cousin hid it in the cave. Nor can you prove that Ms. Chapman stole the original from you."

"Then why are we here?" Emma demanded.

"Because now I know the identity of the ghost knight assailant." Van beckoned to Harriet. "You solved the mystery. It's only right that you take the next step."

Harriet stepped forward. "First, I should apologize for the subterfuge we used to bring you here. But it was important for you to be present. Even though the ghost knight only attacked Ivy and Wes, the rest of you were victims too."

"The ghost knight rearranged the pictures in my office?" Mr. Calabash asked.

"And stole my favorite cookie jar?" Sudden tears appeared in Poppy's eyes, and she dug through her handbag and took out a handkerchief.

"It wasn't my boys?" Ruby said.

At the same time Preston asked, "He rearranged my clothing racks?"

"What's his name?" Mr. Calabash's brown eyes rounded. "It's one of us here, isn't it?"

"Good luck proving any of that," Emma grumbled.

"There's someone here who can recognize the ghost knight," Harriet said, keeping her gaze on Emma.

Skippy Stiles and Jiffy joined Harriet, and Emma flinched but quickly regained her annoyed demeanor.

"You all remember Skippy and Jiffy," Harriet said. "The ghost knight attacked Jiffy too. Unlike us humans, Jiffy doesn't need his eyes to identify his attacker. He has a great sense of smell."

Van pulled an evidence bag from his pocket. "This scrap of material was found in Jiffy's mouth. It's been processed by the crime lab."

Harriet knew from an earlier conversation with Van that DNA had been found on the scrap. All they needed now was to match it to a suspect.

Van handed the evidence bag to Skippy, who removed the fabric and held it in front of Jiffy. "Jiffy, find."

Jiffy had barely gotten to his feet when Emma scurried to stand on top of her chair. "Keep that animal away from me," she shrieked, her eyes filling with tears as Jiffy approached her and emitted a low growl. "Get him away."

Skippy called Jiffy back while Van approached Emma. "Ms. Brinley," he said, his tone formal and authoritative, "would you please roll up your sleeves?"

"No," she howled, still perched on top of the chair. "You can't make me, and I won't. Tell him I won't, Wes."

Instead, Wes took her by the arm. "Knock it off, Emma. The game is over. We lost."

Emma stepped down, her mood belligerent once again. "Keep your mouth shut," she warned.

"I'm not protecting you anymore, Emmie." Wes faced the group. "I'm sorry for what we did. The pranks, I mean, and taking things. It started out as a dare, but then Emma got into a tiff with Poppy, and things escalated. I never meant for anyone to get hurt."

"You hit your head on purpose," Andrew said, his tone a triumphant accusation. "I told you it was self-inflicted."

Emma rolled her eyes. Once again, her arms were crossed, though her stance betrayed her. She wasn't as nonchalant as she had been earlier, and Harriet could almost see steam hissing from her ears.

"Not on purpose," Harriet said, trusting her instinct. "I'm guessing that was an accident."

"Yes," Wes admitted. "I didn't know Emma hurt Ivy until after it happened. We were arguing about it, and Emma pushed me. I fell backward and hit my head. She dialed 999 right before I passed out. Later, when we were alone at hospital, she told me about her brainstorm to frame Heidi. That's all I want to say for now."

As Van, Will, and Mr. Calabash escorted Wes and Emma out of the room in handcuffs, Aunt Jinny approached Harriet and put an arm around her. "You did it," she said quietly. "Another mystery solved."

"I still have questions," Harriet said.

"I'm sure you'll get your answers," Aunt Jinny said. "For now, though, let's put all this behind us and help Ivy get ready for the auction. We must do our best to pull off an extra-special event this year to make up for all she's been through the last few days."

Harriet pulled her aunt into a side hug. "You are a treasure," she said. "Is it any wonder I want to plant my roots next to yours?"

Aunt Jinny gave her a puzzled look. "Haven't you already?"

"Yes. And no." Harriet chuckled. "You're still coming with me to the Whitby Women's Society luncheon tomorrow, aren't you?"

"I wouldn't miss your talk for anything."

"My 'yes and no' will make sense then."

"I'll take your word for it." Aunt Jinny tucked her arm through Harriet's as they made their way to the other end of the pavilion where the auction would take place. "Did I tell you I donated Winston?"

Aunt Jinny's chuckle dispelled the remaining distress Harriet felt about Wes and Emma. She rarely sought out conflict or confrontation, but sometimes neither could be avoided. For now, though, she could put all the misery the cousins had caused behind her and enjoy the evening.

"I'm surprised you'd do that," Harriet replied. "Or that Ivy would allow it."

"She may not know, since I arranged the donation with one of the other volunteers." Aunt Jinny's eyes sparkled with mischief. "It won't amount to much, and Ivy will fuss and fume about what an eyesore it is. But deep down, she'll find it funny."

They found Polly relaxing in a club chair, her ankle propped on a low table, and chatting with Skippy as Jiffy sprawled at his feet. Harriet thanked him profusely. "And you too, Jiffy." She knelt to scratch the border collie's ears. "You're my hero."

"And you're ours," Skippy said. "The way you looked after Jiffy. And me too, when I was feelin' so low. We'll never forget you, lassie."

"Nor I you." Harriet tried to persuade him to stay for the auction, but he had another engagement. After a promise to stop in whenever he was in the area, Skippy said goodbye and headed off with Jiffy.

After they were gone, Aunt Jinny disappeared to talk to someone else, and Harriet sat in the chair next to Polly's. "I owe you an apology."

"For what?"

"I got so excited last night about the possibility of Jiffy identifying the ghost knight that I forgot you had plans with Van today. Why didn't you say something?"

"And miss all this excitement? Never." Polly laughed then gestured toward her foot. "Besides, we'd already decided to postpone the whale-watching excursion until I'm no longer on crutches."

"Any chance of going on a date between now and then?" Harriet asked in a hopeful tone.

Polly's eyes sparkled. "Tonight, actually. Even if he doesn't get back in time for the auction, we're going to dinner afterward."

"Where's he taking you?"

"Actually, I'm taking him. There's this charming little spot I like to call 'Mum's Kitchen.'"

Harriet couldn't believe her ears. "You're going to your parents' house?"

"Scoff all you like, but Mum has already agreed to put something in the oven for us before she and Dad go out on a date of their own. And I'll sit on the couch like the invalid I am and tell Van how to set the table and toss the salad."

"Oh, Polly. There must be something else you can do for your first official date. Something special."

Polly smiled. "Don't you see, Harriet? I've been on countless first dates in my life. Impressive ones. Forgettable ones. In-between ones." She chuckled softly. "Nothing like this though. Van cares more about my comfort and well-being than impressing me. Honestly, he's the one chap I know who'd agree to such a plan. And he acted as if it was the best idea in the world. That alone makes it special. He makes it special."

Harriet beamed at the words. "Then it surely must be. And I hope you have a wonderful evening."

"Thanks. At least we'll have lots to talk about."

Harriet nodded in agreement. She briefly entertained the idea of crashing the tête-à-tête at "Mum's Kitchen" so she'd get her own firsthand account of the Brinley cousins' interrogations. But she couldn't bring herself to barge in on Polly's date.

"And I'll tell you everything I find out tomorrow morning," Polly said, as if she suspected what Harriet had been thinking.

Friends joined them and asked Polly about her injury. As she told them the story, Ivy rushed past. She must have seen Harriet out of the corner of her eye, because she immediately whirled back to speak with her.

"Your umbrella stand is still on display," she said, her tone brisk. "What did you decide to do with it?"

"I'm sorry, Ivy. It completely slipped my mind," Harriet admitted.

"No wonder, with everything else that's been happening." Ivy exhaled a deep breath. "I'm glad the ghost knight is no longer a mystery and we can move on to more important matters. Such as your umbrella stand. Despite the appraisal, I think you could get a decent price for it."

"I'll donate it then." If Aunt Jinny could give up Winston, then Harriet could give up an umbrella stand replica. Even if she loved the story behind the item.

Ivy's eyes widened. "Are you sure?"

"Of course," Harriet said. "My mind is made up. Any and all proceeds can go to the Antique Festival Fund."

"This is most generous of you, Harriet." Ivy grabbed Harriet's hand between both of hers and squeezed it briefly. "Now I must run. So many last-minute details. I'll see you at the auction."

Harriet bit her lip as Ivy hurried away. If Aunt Jinny was wrong and Ivy wasn't amused by Winston's appearance in the auction, then perhaps Harriet's donation of the umbrella stand, which Ivy seemed to love, would offset her irritation.

CHAPTER TWENTY-ONE

After the auction, Harriet joined Will, Aunt Jinny, Ivy, and Sir Halston at a celebratory dinner at the White Hart, where they enjoyed mouthwatering seafood platters and fresh salads. Their primary topic of conversation centered around the arrests of Wes and Emma. Will reported that on the way to the station, Emma broke her silence and tried to pin all the fault on Wes.

"But he is adamant he didn't even know about the attack on Ivy until after it happened," he added. "I tend to believe him."

The pranks started after a minor renovation project had revealed a trapdoor in a back room at Uniquities that opened to an underground tunnel. The curious cousins had followed it a short way up the slope and quickly realized there were similar trapdoors in each of the neighboring shops, but the openings were hidden from above by the flooring.

Wes blamed boredom, and Emma insisted she suffered from inescapable restlessness. Whatever they called it, the result was a series of dares to break into the other stores.

"They figured out where the trapdoors were located for each store. Then one of them would do a reconnaissance mission," Will explained. "Wes actually called it that. They'd go into the store posing as a customer, snoop around, and find out what was on top of the trapdoor. In each instance, it was located in a back room used for storage."

The cousins diligently and carefully figured out ways to cut a large enough space in the flooring for them to squeeze through and then engineered the layer of flooring so the cuts weren't noticeable when it was replaced.

Wes admitted to feeling chuffed when he found Andrew's knight costume at the dry cleaner. That was his first and, he insisted, his lone theft. From then on, the cousins wore it whenever they played their daring game. Emma stole the coral rose cookie jar after she and Poppy argued, and sold it on an online auction site.

"Wes has promised to buy it back no matter the cost," Will added.

All was fun and games as far as the cousins were concerned until Wes promised to exhibit the *Three Dogs at Night* bronze sculpture at the Antique Festival. Emma, who was actually the more skilled at appraisals, knew it was a replica instead of the original, but she hadn't told Wes. Since she couldn't let the experts see it, she managed to steal it back.

When she saw Fern "acting all sneaky" and slipping a note in Ivy's unattended bag at the festival, she read it.

"Emma had followed the tunnel to the cave before," Will said to Ivy. "She hurried home, dressed up in Andrew's costume, and snuck up on you. She was afraid you'd see that someone had been in the cave recently."

Ivy touched the wound on her head. "I didn't hear a thing. My attention was focused on the entrance. What a fool I was."

"Not at all." Sir Halston patted her hand. "You're a romantic, and I find that an admirable trait."

Ivy blushed while Harriet exchanged glances with Aunt Jinny and Will. A love story seemed to be unfolding in front of their very eyes.

By the time dessert came, Will had explained that Emma panicked when Jiffy suddenly appeared, and she'd managed to whack him too. Later, she piled up the rocks to block the tunnel so any searchers wouldn't find where it led, and left herself the secret opening, meaning to return to the cave and retrieve the sculpture for sale later.

When Will finished his story, which had been punctuated with comments and questions from the others, Ivy rested her dessert fork on her plate. "I can add a bit more to the story. Heidi Paxton, of all people, called me earlier. She already knew about the Brinleys' arrests."

"I don't suppose she mentioned where she'd gone." Harriet was still annoyed at how Heidi had left her and Will at the Crow's Nest with the bill.

"She didn't say," Ivy replied. "Not that I expected her to when there's a warrant out for her arrest. But she told me that Uniquities wasn't as profitable as Wes believed. Though Emma had established herself as an astute businesswoman, the truth was that she'd been substituting antiques with replicas for quite some time. Heidi doesn't know the forger's name."

"Does she have any proof of the substitutions?" Aunt Jinny asked. "Why did she call you instead of Van?"

"I asked her the same question, and the simple answer is she doesn't want any contact with the police. Given the circumstances, that's not a surprise. And, yes, she has documentation, which she wants me to give to our dear detective constable."

"At least the mystery of the ghost knight has been solved." Aunt Jinny raised her glass of sparkling cider. "A toast to Harriet and to Will, who did so much to make that happen."

They all raised their glasses, and then Harriet made a toast of her own. "To Aunt Jinny," she said with a mischievous twinkle in her eye. "And to Winston."

Sir Halston let out a hearty chuckle. "Did you have any idea what he was worth?" he asked Aunt Jinny.

"I didn't," Aunt Jinny confessed. "I was just as stunned as everyone else that Fern's boyfriend and that museum agent were in a bidding war for my ugly gargoyle."

"If I hadn't seen it with my own eyes, I'd never have believed it," Ivy declared. "And to think that thing that was in your attic all these years brought in more than ten thousand pounds."

"A hundred times more than my sweet little umbrella stand," Harriet pointed out.

"And much more than its appraisal," Aunt Jinny added.

"Believe me, I no longer trust my own judgment." Ivy reached across the table to squeeze Aunt Jinny's hand. "I know the reason you donated that monstrosity, Jinny Garrett. I'd have played along and pretended to be annoyed while happily taking the money if it had sold for a reasonable price. But if you hadn't donated the gargoyle, you'd be the recipient of that windfall. I almost feel guilty that Lenton Mutter's check isn't going to you."

"A gift is a gift," Aunt Jinny replied. "I'm sure the foundation will put those funds to good use."

"To the foundation," Sir Halston said, and they clinked their glasses once again.

"Will you indulge me in yet another toast?" Will asked. "Ivy was kind to include me in her toast to Harriet. But most of the credit belongs to our devoted veterinarian, who was determined to find the person responsible for harming Ivy and Jiffy. Not only did she keep her promise to Skippy to discover the identity of the ghost knight, but she also found the missing sculpture."

Harriet blushed at the praise. The first phrase of Psalm 84:3, a verse she planned to use in her talk the next day, flitted through her mind. *Even the sparrow has found a home, and the swallow a nest for herself...*

She'd found her home far from where she'd expected to. But in her heart of hearts, she knew that she wouldn't trade the surprises of her days, her interactions with the most unlikely people, and her growing friendships for the life she'd once dreamed about. Connecticut was still home, but so was Yorkshire.

Like the Swedish writer said, she could have more than one home, and she could decide where to plant the roots she carried with her.

Will raised his glass and grinned. "To Dr. Harriet Bailey. The true knight in shining armor in this story. Or, one might say, the Three Dog Knight."

FROM THE AUTHOR

Dear Reader,

In the late 1980s, my family and I lived in Birmingham, England, for about four months.

Because I loved British history—mostly learned from reading historical novels set in England—my heart was near bursting with anticipation as we prepared for this adventure. I truly could not wait to arrive in the UK and get settled in our flat.

We left Florida on a typical hot July day and eventually reached our destination (via plane, bus, and taxi) only to wake up the next morning to a typical not-hot July day. By not-hot, I mean chilly enough I froze in our unheated flat. Because of that and a few other unexpected incidents of culture shock, I experienced a bout of unexpected homesickness that lasted until we headed home again.

Even though I have fond memories of our time there—such as how quickly my then six-year-old and three-year-old daughters learned that cookies were called biscuits and returned to the States with adorable British accents, I've always regretted the cloud I allowed to hang over me.

Those thoughts were with me as I imagined how Harriet might be feeling after a few months away from her Connecticut home, and how her outlook could be both similar and different from mine.

The Henning Mankell quote at the beginning of the book, especially the sentiment that we can carry our roots "and decide where they grow," resonated deeply with me. And not just because of that English experience, but also because I've lived in six different states and a double-digit number of houses in my lifetime.

I waver between being immensely grateful for the blessing of having lived in midwestern rural communities, Florida suburbia, a four-acre patch in a Tennessee cove with a small herd of alpaca, and a major Oklahoma city—experiencing all those geographical and climactic differences—and being envious (yes, I admit it!) of those who've lived most of their lives in one place. Such a blessing it must be to have an intimacy with a community that only comes through years and years of shared experiences, traditions, and heritage.

While Harriet grapples with her homesickness throughout this story, her life becomes ever more entwined with her neighbors and their pets in White Church Bay, and her heart becomes ever more confident about where her roots need to be planted.

Whether you've been a vagabond like me, or you're grappling with homesickness, or your roots are sunk decades-deep into one place, we have this in common—our deepest joy is found in the eternal home that awaits us in heaven.

And until then, we can plant our roots in the place where God directs us with the sure knowledge that His plan is the best plan.

There's nothing unexpected about that!

Signed,
Johnnie Alexander

ABOUT THE AUTHOR

Johnnie Alexander is an award-winning, best-selling novelist of more than twenty works of fiction in a variety of genres. She is on the executive boards of Serious Writer, Inc. and Mid-South Christian Writers Conference and co-hosts an online show called *Writers Chat*.

A fan of classic movies, stacks of books, and road trips, Johnnie shares a life of quiet adventure with Griff, her happy-go-lucky collie, and Rugby, her raccoon-treeing papillon.

A STROLL THROUGH
THE ENGLISH COUNTRYSIDE

Unfortunately, Harriet and Will could only spend a short time in Richmond, a historic market town located in North Yorkshire that was founded in 1071.

The legend of the lost drummer boy has taken such a hold of my imagination that I dream of spending a day or two there myself.

While writing this story, I watched videos of others who followed the path those long-ago soldiers walked from Richmond Castle toward Easby Abbey as they intently listened for the underground beat of the lost drummer boy's drum.

How much I long to make that trek myself—to wander among the abbey's ruins and hike past Easby Woods, to pause for a respectful moment at the memorial marking the place where the drumming stopped, to dip my fingers in the shallow waterfalls of the River Swale, and to explore the eleventh-century castle and its twelfth-century sandstone keep.

Harriet learns a couple variations of the legend, but there's yet another version where King Arthur and his knights are sleeping in a cave beneath the castle. A potter named Thompson accidentally finds them, and as they stir from their slumber, he runs away.

Though neither you nor I can hope to run into Harriet and Will at the fictional Camelot Pub, the dining options in Richmond are plentiful and include cafés and delis, restaurants and takeaways. The Green Howards Museum documents this regiment's history from 1688 to 2006 with over 35,000 items in its collection. And, of course, you can purchase drummer boy souvenirs in the shops.

If you make it to Richmond before I do, please send me a photo of you with the drummer boy stone or the drummer boy statue. Send your photos to the contact page on my website, which you can find by searching my name.

Bonus Info
- All those centuries ago, Richmond was known as Riche Mount, which means "the strong hill."
- The designation of "market town" is an important one. This meant that Richmond was given a royal charter, called a market right, allowing it to hold a market one or two days a week. This charter dates to the Middle Ages.
- One of the largest cobbled squares in England is located in Richmond.

Source: The "potter named Thompson" version of the legend is found in *Folklore, Myths and Legends of Britain* by Russell Ash (Reader's Digest Assoc., Ltd., 1973).

Classic Sausage Rolls

In the US, we have pigs in a blanket. In the UK, this traditional favorite is made with pork sausage instead of miniature hot dogs.

This recipe makes 24 sausage rolls.

Ingredients:

Puff pastry, two sheets

Egg wash (1 large egg, 1 tablespoon of water)

Sausage filling:

1 pound ground pork sausage

1 tablespoon finely chopped fresh thyme

1 tablespoon Worcestershire sauce

½ teaspoon ground sage

½ teaspoon onion powder

½ teaspoon ground pepper (black or white)

Toasted fennel seeds (optional)

Directions:

1) Unless you *love* making your own puff pastry, it's fine to use the premade variety. If frozen, thaw two sheets at room temperature.

2) Preheat oven to 400 degrees.

3) Line baking sheet with parchment paper.

4) Create egg wash by whisking egg with water. Set aside.

5) Combine all ingredients listed above for sausage filling.

6) Refrigerate sausage filling mixture for at least 15 minutes (until firm).

7) Prepare puff pastry:

   a) Lightly flour cutting board and roll each sheet into 9×10-inch rectangle.

   b) Cut each sheet in half, lengthwise, to create total of 4 rectangles measuring 4.5×10 inches.

8) Construct the sausage rolls:

   a) Divide sausage mixture into four equal portions.

   b) Roll each portion into 10-inch log.

9) Create one roll at a time:

   a) Place sausage log in middle of pastry rectangle.

   b) Brush egg wash over edges of pastry.

   c) Wrap pastry over log and carefully seal seam. (Leave ends open.)

   d) Cut each roll into six equal slices.

   e) Place slices, seam-side down and about inch apart, on baking sheet.

10) Once all slices have been prepared and placed on baking sheet, brush tops with remaining egg wash.

11) Bake 12 minutes. Rotate baking sheet.

12) Bake 8 to 12 more minutes (or until pastry is golden brown and sausage is cooked all the way through). Cool on wire rack for about 5 minutes.

13) Serve with your favorite dipping sauces. A few suggestions:

   a) Chutney

   b) Honey mustard

   c) BBQ sauce

   d) Your favorite condiment!

*Read on for a sneak peek of another exciting book
in the* Mysteries of Cobble Hill Farm *series!*

Show Stopper

BY SHIRLEY RAYE REDMOND

Lord Peter Wimsey is fit as a fiddle." Harriet Bailey made the happy pronouncement as she rubbed her hands along the back of a well-groomed Scottish terrier. His coat was black and wiry, his dark eyes twinkling, his nose cold and wet. When she gave him a scratch behind his left ear, the little terrier leaned into her hand, wagging his tail as if to thank her.

Harriet went on. "I'm sure he'll perform well at the dog show. It wouldn't surprise me one bit if he wins Best in Show."

The dog's owner, a short, fiftysomething woman named Gwen Higginbottom, beamed her thanks, her cheeks pink with pleasure. She had dark hair generously streaked with gray. Her blue sweater— or jumper, as they called it here—made her blue eyes appear particularly bright. "Do you really think so? You're not just saying that to be kind?"

"I really think so," Harriet assured her.

"Petey is a handsome lad, if I do say so myself," Gwen agreed. With a dry chuckle, she added, "He's got a mind of his own, and he's cheeky too, but he's the best dog I've ever owned. Took to the show ring like a pro, even when he was a pup. I was so proud when he won Best in Breed at the regional competition that I nearly burst my buttons." She regarded her pet fondly. "You're the apple of my eye, aren't you, Petey dear?"

Lord Peter, fondly called Petey by those who knew him best, seemed to preen under the attention. Harriet felt certain the dog understood that he was being praised. As she lifted him down from the examination table, she could easily see why he had won competitions in Yorkshire and beyond. Solid and compact with erect ears, a perky tail, and piercing black eyes, the Scottie was a perfect example of his breed.

"He's a dapper little lad." Harriet tried to employ words she referred to as "Yorkshire-isms." It hadn't been easy to learn the different words and expressions used by her British neighbors. She still made plenty of mistakes.

Fortunately, Polly Thatcher, the vet clinic receptionist, was proving to be an able and willing tutor. Harriet was now used to filling her vehicle's tank with petrol instead of gas, and she knew that a biscuit was really a cookie, not something warm and fluffy to smother with sausage gravy. It took some getting used to after more than thirty years of American terminology, but Harriet felt confident she'd get there. She was already familiar with many of the differences after the summer vacations she'd spent with her grandfather growing up.

Polly came into the room with a dog treat, which she offered to Petey. The Scottie sniffed it with a twitch of his little black nose before gently taking it from her outstretched hand. "Isn't he posh in that plaid collar and matching lead?" Polly asked. "The entire village will be rooting for this little man, won't we now?"

Petey wagged his tail, turning adoring eyes on Polly.

Harriet felt her lips quirk up at the corners. It didn't surprise her that Petey had fallen under Polly's spell. Until she'd begun to date the local constable, the attractive, spunky young woman had half the single men in White Church Bay dogging her heels—pun intended. The animals that visited the clinic all loved her too, as did their owners. Polly had a way of putting those around her at ease.

"I'll admit I'm more than a little antsy," Gwen said. "My stomach is all in knots when I think about the show. I always get fidgety before a competition, but this is the big one. It's being televised, which makes me even more nervous."

"Of course you're nervous," Polly said. "With everyone watching on the telly. Still, we'll all be so proud when Petey takes the top prize. You can count on it."

Gwen turned anxious eyes to Harriet. "Do you think I should have my hair and makeup done? I want to appear professional during the performance, but not overdone. I have to choose my wardrobe carefully. Whatever I wear must be comfortable, especially my shoes, so I can take Petey through his paces without worrying about twisting my ankle or something."

"That makes sense." Harriet hadn't realized there were so many things to take into consideration while prepping for a dog show. One had to do much more than simply show up with a dog and leash.

"Here's hoping our Petey doesn't flop down in the middle of the ring and demand a tummy rub instead of going through his routine," Polly quipped.

Harriet laughed at the mental image, but Gwen responded with an anxious, "Oh dear."

"Petey's a pro," Harriet reminded her. "You'll do fine, and so will he."

Gwen had never married or raised children. Dogs were her life. For years she'd poured all her attention and affection into her terriers. Harriet knew that Gwen was as proud of Petey as any mother might be of her child.

"Petey's well trained and in good health. There's nothing to be nervous about, Gwen. You'll both give it your best, and everything will work out the way it's supposed to." Harriet patted the woman's shoulder.

"That's right," Polly agreed. "Petey won't embarrass you. He never has before, has he?"

"There's a first time for everything." Gwen's grim reply was followed by a shudder.

A few years ago, Harriet's late grandfather, Dr. Harold Bailey, had painted a picture of Petey as a young pup. It was one of the best animal portraits he'd ever done, in Harriet's opinion. He'd captured the lively personality of the confident little terrier, his joyful, independent spirit reflected in the gleam of his dark eyes. It appeared as if Petey had actually smiled for his portrait.

Harriet had to admit, if only to herself, that Petey was one of her favorite patients. Feeling slightly disloyal at the thought, she glanced about for Maxwell, wondering where the little dachshund had gotten to. Though his back legs had been paralyzed when he had been hit by a car, the office mascot was quite mobile in a wheeled prosthesis Harriet's grandfather had acquired for him.

He was probably near Polly's desk, under the watchful eye of Charlie, the office cat. Charlie had been rescued from a burning dustbin as a kitten, leaving her with patchy muted-calico fur. What she lacked in beauty, she made up for in cleverness and a sweet temperament. She was the latest in a long line of office cats named Charlie regardless of gender, a tradition Old Doc Bailey had insisted gave him one less thing to remember.

Realizing that Gwen was watching her, Harriet added another word of encouragement. "As Polly said, everyone in the village will be cheering for you and Petey."

"You're going to be famous, little Petey," Polly said, ruffling the dog's ears. To Gwen she added, "Will you stay in a grand London hotel? I didn't think they allowed pets in their establishments."

Gwen brushed a loose strand of hair from her face. "The ones catering to the dog show crowd happily do so. They offer special rates and even treats for the dogs."

"You know, Gwen, if Petey wins the grand championship, you may become swamped with requests for stud service," Harriet pointed out. "Are you prepared for that?"

"Certainly." Gwen chuckled. "It's about time this little guy earned his keep."

The sound of a bell over the clinic's front door and a man's gruff voice calling out from the waiting room interrupted their conversation. Polly went to greet the newcomer, and Harriet said to Gwen, "My next patient is here. Do you have any other questions for me?"

"No, but I believe I recognize that voice. It's Rupert Decker, isn't it?"

"Yes, he called earlier this morning to see if I could look at Ivanhoe, his German shepherd."

Gwen held up a forefinger. "We call them Alsatians around here, just so you know."

"Thank you." Now that Gwen brought it up Harriet recalled her aunt Jinny mentioning that many British people had refused to call the breed German shepherds since World War I.

Tipping her head toward the outer office, Gwen murmured, "Ivanhoe is a fine dog, but I can't say I like the man all that much. I hired him to build some shelves in my spare room a short time ago, and I must say he did a poor job. He also didn't like it at all when I made him come back to remount them. Besides, he's rude. He said some unkind things that I won't repeat." Gwen lowered her eyes, adding in a small voice, "He actually frightened me at the time. In a way, he still does."

"Has he threatened you in any way?" Harriet asked.

Gwen released a slow breath. "No."

Had she hesitated before replying? Harriet couldn't be sure.

She'd met Rupert Decker once before in the village. He was surly, tall, and lean, with short, grizzled whiskers that gave the impression he'd forgotten to shave for a day or two. He'd freely told her he didn't like vets or doctors, so she'd been quite surprised when he'd called to make an appointment for his dog.

All the same, he was concerned enough about Ivanhoe to have Harriet examine the dog. That was a point in his favor. Harriet couldn't abide people who neglected their animals.

"If you need some carpentry work done around your place, I'd advise you to find someone other than Mr. Decker," Gwen said.

"I'll bear it in mind," Harriet replied. Sensing that Gwen would prefer not to pass the surly carpenter and his dog in the reception area, she suggested that they make their exit through her house, which was attached to the clinic.

The woman's face exhibited relief. "How kind of you. Petey does forget he's a pint-size dog. I wouldn't want him to antagonize an Alsatian."

After Gwen was on her way, Harriet mustered her best smile and greeted the newcomer. "Good afternoon, Mr. Decker. What seems to be the problem with Ivanhoe today?" She held out her hand to the large dog, allowing him to sniff her. Once the dog accepted this familiarity, Harriet gave him a welcoming pat on the head.

"He's limping, that's what. Something wrong with his foot or maybe his leg. Can't tell," Rupert Decker said, rising from the chair. He wore a corduroy jacket and a squashed cap. "He growls whenever I try to see it for myself. Figured I'd bring him in and see what you can do about it. You're the expert, so maybe you can help him without getting yourself chewed up in the process."

Harriet and Polly exchanged a glance. Was it possible the grumpy man was afraid of his own dog?

The sound of a car starting outside attracted Rupert's attention. He scowled out the window. "Is that the old Higginbottom busybody sneaking away?"

Harriet ignored the remark and asked him to bring Ivanhoe into an exam room. She watched the dog's gait, recognizing immediately that something was wrong with his front left paw. Perhaps he had a splinter. "Would you like to return to the reception area, Mr. Decker, and have a seat? Polly and I can handle Ivanhoe."

"You think so? He's a big dog, not like that squirt of Higginbottom's."

Harriet resisted the urge to roll her eyes. She'd cared for horses, cows, donkeys, and even llamas. A dog was hardly going to be a problem, even a larger one like an Alsatian. She kept her tone even. "We'll get along fine, won't we, Ivanhoe?"

"I'll stay and watch all the same," Rupert said.

"Suit yourself," Harriet replied as Polly handed her a muzzle of the appropriate size. Ivanhoe had given no indication that he might bite, but any dog could nip when injured, and she didn't know this one yet. The muzzle was a precaution to keep both of them safe.

Harriet made a few other necessary preparations and then rolled a stool in front of the dog. After donning a pair of disposable gloves, she sat down and examined her patient, talking to him in quiet, soothing tones. With disinfectant, sterilized tweezers, and a skill born of considerable experience, she removed a large thorn from Ivanhoe's paw pad, praising him for his bravery. Then she wrapped a stretchy blue bandage around his foot. It wouldn't stay on long, but it would protect the wound for a little while.

"There, all done." She patted the dog's head and flashed Rupert a smile as she removed the muzzle.

When Polly offered the dog a treat, Rupert snorted and muttered something under his breath. The man then mumbled his thanks in a rather reluctant manner.

Harriet replied with a crisp, "You're welcome."

When he followed Polly into the outer office to pay the bill, Harriet tidied the exam rooms and listened to Rupert leave the clinic. She thought again about Petey and realized she resented the man for calling Petey a squirt. The terrier was a bona fide champion. Even if he didn't win the big dog show in London, he had won other competitions. And his charm would always make him a champion in her book.

Harriet had opened a cabinet to check on her supply of disinfectant wipes and alcohol swabs when Polly poked her head into the room. "Van is here. In his official capacity, I might add. He says he has a new mystery for you."

A NOTE FROM THE EDITORS

We hope you enjoyed another exciting volume in the Mysteries of Cobble Hill Farm series, published by Guideposts. For over seventy-five years, Guideposts, a nonprofit organization, has been driven by a vision of a world filled with hope. We aspire to be the voice of a trusted friend, a friend who makes you feel more hopeful and connected.

By making a purchase from Guideposts, you join our community in touching millions of lives, inspiring them to believe that all things are possible through faith, hope, and prayer. Your continued support allows us to provide uplifting resources to those in need. Whether through our communities, websites, apps, or publications, we inspire our audiences, bring them together, and comfort, uplift, entertain, and guide them. Visit us at guideposts.org to learn more.

We would love to hear from you. Write us at Guideposts, P.O. Box 5815, Harlan, Iowa 51593 or call us at (800) 932-2145. Did you love *Three Dog Knight*? Leave a review for this product on guideposts.org/shop. Your feedback helps others in our community find relevant products.

Find inspiration, find faith, find Guideposts.
Shop our best sellers and favorites at
guideposts.org/shop
Or scan the QR code to go directly to our Shop

Find more inspiring stories in these best-loved Guideposts fiction series!

Mysteries of Lancaster County

Follow the Classen sisters as they unravel clues and uncover hidden secrets in Mysteries of Lancaster County. As you get to know these women and their friends, you'll see how God brings each of them together for a fresh start in life.

Secrets of Wayfarers Inn

Retired schoolteachers find themselves owners of an old warehouse-turned-inn that is filled with hidden passages, buried secrets, and stunning surprises that will set them on a course to puzzling mysteries from the Underground Railroad.

Tearoom Mysteries Series

Mix one stately Victorian home, a charming lakeside town in Maine, and two adventurous cousins with a passion for tea and hospitality. Add a large scoop of intriguing mystery, and sprinkle generously with faith, family, and friends, and you have the recipe for *Tearoom Mysteries*.

Ordinary Women of the Bible

Richly imagined stories—based on facts from the Bible—have all the plot twists and suspense of a great mystery, while bringing you fascinating insights on what it was like to be a woman living in the ancient world.

To learn more about these books, visit Guideposts.org/Shop